Science, Technology, and Latin American Narrative in the Twentieth Century and Beyond

Jerry Hoeg

Lehigh
University
Press

Bethlehem: Lehigh University Press
London: Associated University Presses

Associated University Presses
440 Forsgate Drive
Cranbury, NJ 08512

Associated University Presses
16 Barter Street
London WC1A 2AH, England

Associated University Presses
P.O. Box 338, Port Credit
Mississauga, Ontario
Canada L5G 4L8

The paper used in this publication meets the requirements
of the American National Standard for Permanence of Paper
for Printed Library Materials Z39.48–1984.

Library of Congress Cataloging-in-Publication Data

Hoeg, Jerry, 1951–
    Science, technology, and Latin American narrative in the twentieth century and
    beyond / Jerry Hoeg.
        p. cm.
    Includes bibliographical references and index.
    ISBN 0-934223-61-0 (alk. paper)
    1. Spanish American fiction—20th century—History and criticism. 2. Postmodernism
(Literature)—Latin America. 3. Science in literature. 4. Technology in literature. 5.
Literature and science—Latin America. 6. Literature and society—Latin America. I.
Title.

PQ7082.N7 H64 2000
863'.609356—dc21   00-201178

PRINTED IN THE UNITED STATES OF AMERICA

Contents

Acknowledgments

At great risk of offending those I shall not mention by name, I would like to single out for special thanks a few of the multitude who have helped me on this project. First and foremost, of course, Adriene, for her infinite patience, without which none of this would have been possible.

I would like to thank Justo Alarcón and Teresa Valdivieso for getting me started on this path, and Carl Mitcham for his help in thinking through many of the ideas in this book. I should also like to express my gratitude to everyone at the Ometeca Institute, but especially to Rafael Catalá, Luis Jiménez, and Kevin Larsen. And lastly, Japan's leading specialist on Brazilian culture, Eva Bueno, provided invaluable insights and inspiration.

Finally, I wish to thank the editors of various journals first for publishing my work, and secondly for allowing me to use the material in this book. Portions of the following articles have been incorporated into the book, at times verbatim, and in other instances in revised form. An earlier version of chapter 3 appeared in *Mosaic*, volume 30/4, pp. 95–108; an earlier version of chapter 4 appeared in *Confluencia*, 12/2, pp. 112–27; and a previous version of chapter 4 was published in *Revista Canadiense de Estudios Hispánicos* 20/3, pp. 491–504. The tables on *mestizaje* that appear in chapter 5 are reproduced, with slight changes, from *The Latin Americans: Contemporary Peoples and Their Cultural Traditions* by Michael D. Olien (1973) by Holt, Rinehart and Winston, reprinted by permission of the publisher. Sections of chapter 5 are taken from an article entitled "Cultural Counterpoint: Antonio Benítez Rojo's Postmodern Transculturation" that appeared in the *Journal of Latin American Cultural Studies* 6/1, pp. 65–75. Parts of chapter 6 are from "Myth, Modernity, and Postmodern Tragedy in Walter Lima's *The Dolphin*" published in *Imagination Beyond Nation: Latin American Popular Culture* (1998), Eva Paulino Bueno and Terry Caesar, eds., pp. 195–209, used by permission of the University of Pittsburgh Press.

One part of chapter 7 appeared in an earlier form in *Estudios en honor de Janet Pérez* (1998), Susana A. Cavallo, Luis A. Jiménez, and Oralia Preble-Niemi, eds., pp 61–74, by Scripta Humanistica. Finally, the two poems that appear in chapter 8 are reprinted by permission of the author, Rafael Catalá.

Introduction

My central purpose in writing this book was to stimulate interest in the role of humanistic studies in deciding how science and technology impact Latin America. My motivation was the simple observation that while science and technology have always had an enormous impact on both humanity and nature in Latin America, mainstream literary criticism in and about Latin America has generally sought to separate itself from and, essentially, ignore the sciences, an approach not without its repercussions. Interestingly enough, creative writers and other artists in Latin America, those who produce the humanistic narrative of the region, have been anything but silent on the subject of science and technology. From Sor Juana Inés de la Cruz (1651–1695) and Carlos de Sigüenza y Góngora (1645–1700) to Jorge Luis Borges (1899–1986), Octavio Paz (1914–1998), and Ernesto Cardinal (1925–   ), Latin American writers have maintained an ongoing dialogue with science. If we accept that their creative production has had an effect on the way science and technology are perceived in Latin America, and that this perception has altered the impact of science and technology in Latin America, then the stories creative people tell about science and technology are very much worth looking at. That they are indeed worth contemplating is the essential premise of this book.

For methodological purposes, this study takes as its point of departure the proposition that society and culture are, among many other things, communications systems. From this it follows that they must have a coding or redundancy that protects them from the perturbations of a noisy environment. In any communication system, the code mediates all messages between participants, and so allows the participants to distinguish between systemic messages and environmental perturbations, between information and noise, between order and disorder. If one wishes to understand the messages, one must understand the code. The question is, if one wishes to change the messages, must one change the code?

I have chosen to call the code that mediates contemporary sociocultural relations, at least in the West and probably universally, the Social Imaginary. I do not suggest that this is a stable, nonchanging, arrangement, always the same in all times and all places, but I do assert that there exist essential and recurrent features which have come to the fore with a vengeance in our present age. These features, such as instrumental reason, the concept of infinite progress, and the technoscientific domination of humanity and nature are, in critiques from Marx, Weber, and Durkhiem through the Frankfort school and on to Habermas and Lyotard, generally equated with Modernity. Moreover, following Martin Heidegger, Friedreich Nietzsche, and José Ortega y Gasset, I would argue that many of these distinctive features of Modernity can be found at least as early classical Greece. In any case, this study concentrates on the twentieth century, one in which technoscientific Modernity can be said to be in full flower.[1]

The mediating code or enframing of Modernity produces various messages or discourses. An initial function of this book, then, is to consider the relation between the Social Imaginary and the various scientific discourses it produces. A subsequent goal is to look at the ways in which these technoscientific discourses are represented in selected examples of Hispanic literature and film. This approach assumes science and culture are very much interrelated through their mutual mediation by the Social Imaginary. By means of a transdisciplinary investigation of these discourses it is hoped a better understanding of the sociocultural construction, and possible reconstruction, of these discourses can be realized. The ultimate aim of this inquiry is to shed light on the possibility of constructing alternative codes or mediations which will produce sociotechnical messages of empowerment rather than domination. In other words, the book is about change. If one is not happy with the present state of affairs, where does one begin to effect real change, and not just cosmetic modifications that are promptly co-opted by the system? How are science and technology part of the problem and how are they part of the solution? What is the role of cultural expression in determining the uses of technology? How do the sciences and the humanities affect each other, and how are they constrained by, and how can they effectively contest, the Social Imaginary? Through a transdisciplinary approach, this book hopes to offer a point of departure for a different type of discussion of these and related questions.

The first chapter deals with the mediation of both theory and technics in the West since ancient Greece. Drawing primarily on works of Heidegger and Ortega, this chapter looks at how everyday technics or uses of technology are mediated by theoretical knowledge. This chapter argues that theoretical knowledge is itself a message mediated by the Western Social Imaginary, and so in order to understand our present social relationships (messages) one must understand the higher level coding that mediates them. Both Heidegger and Ortega, albeit in different manners, assert that the essence of our present technological era is nothing technological, but rather the product of a higher level mediation. Heidegger calls this mediation *das Ge-stell*, while Ortega refers to it as the social construction or definition of *bienestar* or well-being. An important point made by both these philosophers of technology is that the coding which produces the present social relations between society and technology is not a stable, fixed affair, but rather merely one possibility among many, and so subject to recodification should the participants in the system so desire. Alternative social mediations are discussed, as are the formal requirements for change in any communication system.

In the second chapter, the nature of the mediation of scientific discourse in Latin American narrative is examined. This second level mediation, which is itself a message constrained by the overarching Social Imaginary discussed in chapter one, is shown to have played a primary role in Latin American narrative from its beginnings up to the present day. This chapter offers an overview of some recurrent images of science, scientists, and technology seen in Latin American fiction. Through an analysis of three novels—Gabriel García Márquez's *One Hundred Years of Solitude* (1971), Isabel Allende's *The House of the Spirits* (1986), and Jorge Amado's *Gabriela, Clove and Cinnamon* (1974)—this chapter seeks to outline the nature of the debate over the uses of technology in Latin America, especially as it plays out in fiction, and to stress the importance of considering the mediation of both the Social Imaginary and the discourses of theoretical science when assessing the literary representations of this debate.

Chapter three, through an analysis of Laura Esquivel's *Like Water for Chocolate* (1990), takes an in-depth look at one recurrent view of science and technology in Latin America. This perspective equates patriarchal technoscience with foreign domination and seeks to contrast this type of knowledge with a more feminine, indigenous, and truly Latin American way of knowing and being.

Chapter four, by means of an appraisal of the Costa Rican author Fernando Contreras Castro's *Unica mirando al mar* (1993), seeks to elucidate the mediation of various scientific discourses—natural science, anthropology, ecology—as these are represented in the novel, and to situate this scientific mediation in relation to current debates in social theory on the nature of modernity and postmodernity, popular and mass culture, and science and technology in contemporary Latin American society.

The fifth chapter deals with Antonio Benítez Rojo's use of recent scientific theories, such as complexity theory and chaos theory, to elucidate an old problem in Latin America, namely that of racial and ethnic strife. From the *Raza cósmica* of José Vasconcelos to the Cuban counterpoint of Fernando Ortiz and on to Benítez Rojo's postmodern transculturation, this chapter examines the relations between race, ethnicity, literature and scientific theory.

The next chapter, the sixth, treats visual narrative, specifically the Brazilian director Walter Lima's film *The Dolphin* (1987). This chapter examines some of the theories that underlie postmodern visual narrative in Latin America, from the Oedipal to the ethnographic, including Candace Slater's classic *Dance of the Dolphin* (1994). A central question addressed is that of whether a postmodern multiplicity of narratives is liberatory and/or produces what René Girard calls a crisis of distinctions.

The seventh chapter treats the arrival of the "new media" in Latin American literary production, and the related question of whether a new medium will produce a new message. This chapter looks at both theoretical and creative production regarding literature and multimedia in the Spanish-speaking world.

The final chapter looks at three representative works or, perhaps better, three bodies of work, in an attempt to provide an overview of some of the many representations of science and technology found in Latin American creative production. The chapter ends by emphasizing the importance of considering not only what these discourses say, but also what they do in terms of influencing the impact of science and technology in Latin America. This book is not meant to be, nor is it, complete in any way. It is certainly not intended to replace any other approach, nor indeed, do the essays herein represent a unified approach. In fact, quite to the contrary, these essays trace a number of possible avenues through which to approach an undeniable reality, namely the powerful, evergrowing and, it would seem, nearly omnipresent influence of science and technology in the lived experience of the vast majority of human beings. It has been said that we must not leave the future in the hands of the scientists (Harding 1986; Sarlo 1994). I'm not altogether sure I agree. To accept this view is to perpetuate the metaphysics of the intellectual division of labor. The discourse of science is not hegemonic, and it is not humanity's 'fate' to be modern. There are voices coming from within the sciences that have at least as much to offer as those that are heard in literature. In the final analysis, this book simply seeks to suggest that both scientists and humanists have much to say to each other about where we are now, where we might wish to go, and what we need to do to get there. Perhaps a transdisciplinary fusion will permit the participants in the system to escape the identities imposed upon them, and so enable the construction of a new, and as yet unthinkable social mediation, that turning away from our current enframing described by Heidegger as "the arrival of another destining that does not allow itself to be either logically or historically predicted or to be metaphysically construed as a sequence belonging to a process of history" (Heidegger 1977, 39). This book suggests the first step in a turning away from our enframing is to know the nature of that enframing.

Science, Technology, and Latin American Narrative in the Twentieth Century and Beyond

1
Taking Responsibility

> But where danger is, grows
> The saving power also.
> —Hölderlin

In the final decades of the twentieth century, the supposedly objective nature of modern science has begun to be systematically questioned. Numerous scholars, in a variety of fields, have demonstrated the socially constructed nature of the so-called "value free" sciences. The central thrust of this movement has been to emphasize the degree to which the values of a given society are reflected in its science, the degree to which science is an artifact of a given social milieu. Conversely, scholars have also begun to focus on the influence of science in the construction of both social and narrative texts.

If we accept that both literary and scientific discourse are products of a given sociocultural context, then we should reasonably expect to find mutual influences or reciprocal relations between the two discourses. If this is indeed the case, then it follows that literature not only reflects the discourse of science and technology, but also has the power to change the social milieu and hence technological practice. From this there arises the question of responsibility, of the possible role of literature in reconstructing the discourses of technology. In her "Cyborg Manifesto" Donna Haraway explains what this might entail: "Taking responsibility for the social relations of science and technology means refusing an anti-science metaphysics, a demonology of technology, and so means embracing the *skilful task of reconstructing the boundaries of daily life*, in partial connection with others, in communication with all our parts" (Haraway 1991b, 181; emphasis mine). It is the possibility of our taking responsibility for the social relations of science and technology, the nature of this ongoing reconstruction, and the role of literature in this process that I seek to explore.

17

This initial chapter seeks to trace the possible feedback loops between what Cornelius Castoriadis terms the "Social Imaginary" and defines as the ultimate locus of mediation of all societal relations or messages (Castoriadis 1987, 115–64), and three of the fields mediated by the Social Imaginary. These three areas are: Western science, taken as an ensemble of privileged, "objective," and empirically oriented theories of the real; modern technology in the sense of the rational organization and use of tools, technics, and humans designed to produce optimum efficiency; creative production, including literature and film. It is hoped that an understanding of these feedback loops will make possible a more thorough evaluation of the possible influence of literature in transforming the Social Imaginary and hence the discourses mediated by it, especially the dominating versions of the discourses of science and technology which, by positing the relation between society and nature as one of binary competition, have produced disastrous results for both humanity and the environment, particularly in the Third World.

If feedback loops exist between literature and the Social Imaginary, then so too does the possibility of constructing scientific and technological discourses which empower humanity to co-evolve a symbiotic system-environment relation with the rest of nature, both organic and inorganic. This symbiotic relation would require a different kind of mediation, a "Social Symbolic" rather than a Social Imaginary. Here, I use the term Social Symbolic not in the Lacanian sexual-linguistic sense, but rather to refer to a form of mediation that transcends the competitive relations of binary opposition produced in the Imaginary. The Social Symbolic, in my sense of the term, generates messages that may signify different things in different contexts, but that are always symbolic of cooperative and sustainable long-term relations between system and environment. Importantly, then, there is often a distinction between what these discourses say and what they do.

Few would contest the proposition that the Western Social Imaginary is intimately linked to concepts such as analytic logic, reason, and infinite progress and perfectibility. Many have traced the lineage of this particular form of ordering the world, modernity if you will, to the origins of Western thought in classical Greece. Thus Nietzsche equates the rise of pure reason with the Socratic elenchus and Friedreich Schlegel finds the concept of infinite perfectibility already in place in Pythagoras.[1] Following the same intellectual tradition, Max Weber highlights the later institutionalization of instrumental reason, wherefore its propensity toward domination, and Theodor Adorno argues that the objectifying nature of scientific reason leads finally to the objectification and domination of human beings.[2]

According to Martin Heidegger, who stands at the apex of this line of thought, the establishment of Reason as the sole arbiter of truth begins with Platonic metaphysics, a theoretical move designed to ensure the separation of subject from object. By Heidegger's account, this original metaphysical move produces a social enframing or *Ge-stell* whose eventual product is the modern technological world—Modernity—which is the culmination of Western metaphysics:

> Modern technology pursues the maximum possible perfection. Perfection consists in the calculability, without exception, of objects. The calculability of objects presupposes the unlimited validity of the "principium rationis." The domination, already characterized, of the principle of reason determines the being of the modern epoch, of the technological era. (Heidegger 1983, 79)

For Heidegger, das *Ge-stell* names the precondition of modern technology, a way of ordering the world that ultimately produces a science of technics—technology—but that is not, in itself, technological: "*Ge-stell* refers to the mode of revealing that rules in the essence of modern technology and is not itself anything technological" (Heidegger 1977, 20).

As mentioned above, Heidegger traces this mediation back to ancient Greek techno-productivist metaphysics, Plato's concept of *eidos* as eternal blueprint or theoretical model from which the sensible world is produced (Zimmerman 1990, 168). Consequently, for Heidegger, a certain mode of enframing the world precedes technology which, in turn, precedes science (Ihde 1983). Importantly, this enframing or *Ge-stell* mediates not only technology, but also the ontologically prior domain of technics. This means that not only the discourse of science and technology falls under the sway of the metaphysical *Ge-stell*, but indeed all socio-cultural relationships or "doing." Therefore, the enframing or coding of the Social Imaginary mediates the messages of both science and literature, and so provides the continuity that links these two discursive branches on the family tree of Modernity.

In Hispanic letters, the leading philosopher of technology is José Ortega y Gasset. Writing in approximately the same period as Heidegger, Ortega, principally in "Meditación de la técnica" ("Meditation on Technics") and "El mito del hombre allende de la técnica" ("The Myth of Man Beyond Technics") outlines his view of the relation between humanity and technics. For Ortega, human existence is not limited to the initial conditions as given in the natural world, but rather is capable first of imagining conditions beyond those given by organic and inorganic nature, and second of organizing undertakings whose goal is to realize the projects initially conceived in the imagination. These imagined projects can be spiritual or material, and are realized through various kinds of technics or ways of doing. For Ortega, human life involves a relationship with the circumstances of the natural world in which human beings play an active role in creating, responding to, and realizing these circumstances. Technics is the key to the material realization of creative (and so originally imaginary) attitudes toward the world. Technics is "the reform that man imposes on nature in view of the satisfaction of his necessities" (Ortega 1945–47b, 324). Moreover, the goal of these projects, the true human necessity, is not that of mere physical existence, but rather spiritual fulfillment. According to Ortega, humankind does not desire simply *estar* (simple physical existence), but rather *bienestar* (physical and spiritual well-being):

> life signifies for Man not simple existence, but living well. . . . Living well
> and not simply existing is the fundamental necessity for Man, the necessity
> of necessities. (Ortega 1945–47b, 328)

A key distinction between the view postulated by Ortega and that adumbrated by Heidegger concerns the role of technics in human socio-cultural activity.[3] For Heidegger, the imposition of a certain metaphysical enframing or *Ge-stell*—the Social Imaginary—is an essential feature of the Western human condition which leads inevitably to our current technological society. For Ortega, on the other hand, the technics used to realize the creative projects of humanity can also lead to symbolic rather that imaginary constructions, that is, to cultural messages, such as art or literature, which can produce a society whose relations with the real are not predominantly rationalist or metaphysical. Although Ortega's view of technics is primarily anthropological/instrumental (a means to an end), he does not posit a determinist *telos* other than *bienestar*. According to Ortega in *Meditación de la técnica*:

> That which Man calls living, living well or *bienestar* is a term that is always
> mobile, unlimitedly variable. And as the repertoire of human necessities is a
> function of it, these too are no less variable, and because technology is the
> repertoire of acts provoked, roused *by* and inspired *in* the system of these
> necessities, it is also a proteiform reality, in constant mutation. Therefore, it
> is futile to want to study technology as an independent entity or as if it were
> directed by a unique vector which is known prior to investigation. (Ortega
> 1945–47b, 330)

While the desire for *bienestar* is an essential feature of humanity, the definition of *bienestar* is not fixed, but is instead the fruit (bitter or sweet) of social negotiation.

An important corollary of Ortega's nondeterminist model is the idea that *bienestar* is realized through practices, in doing, in an active response to and creation of circumstances, and not in pure theory or "*la técnica*," Ortega's version of Heidegger's *das Ge-stell*: "life is fundamentally not as so many centuries have believed: contemplation, thought, theory. No; it is production, fabrication" (Ortega 1945–47b, 341–42).

From this, several possibilities emerge. First of all, if a given society changes its system of necessities, its definition of bienestar, then that society's *repertorio* of technics must also change. The necessities of the system are messages mediated by the coding of the Social Imaginary. If the code changes, so must the messages or perceived necessities. Conversely, if the context in which a society functions changes, it can maintain its present *Ge-stell* either through intensification of existing technologies, changing its assortment of technics, or both.[4]

If social production or fabrication changes, however, so also may social coding. On this view, alternative technics or ways of doing have the saving power to change the Code if they indeed produce *bienestar*. In this way, in a Lamarckian sense, change can travel from the message level of social actions to the mediating level of the social code. The cyberneticist Gregory Bateson called this process "somatic adaptation," and cited by way of example the legislative process wherein first a change is made and accepted by the people, and only later codified as law (Bateson 1989, 354).

In hindsight, we can see, as recent anthropological studies have shown, that the possibility of alternative technosocial paradigms was not merely idle speculation on Ortega's part. There are indeed many societies that have subordinated technics to a symbolic mediation of their relation with the Real.

Roy A. Rappaport's study of the Tsembaga of New Guinea in *Pigs for the Ancestors* elucidates one such society. The Tsembaga cosmology revolves around two sets of spirits, the Red Spirits and the Spirits of Rot. These spirits are said to represent dead ancestors, to whom the living owe abiding obligations, principally for aiding the living in time of war. Meeting the symbolic debt to the ancestors requires an ongoing cycle of ritualized warfare and pig sacrifice. The cycle also involves a variety of taboos on certain foods, sexual intercourse, and so on. According to Rappaport (1969), it is due to the mediation of the cosmological system "that the actual material variables comprising the ecosystem are regulated" (254). The net effect of the six- to twenty-year cycle of pig production, pig sacrifice, ritual warfare, and return to pig production, with its accompanying taboos, is to provide a sustainable balance between human population and the carrying capacity of the valley in which the approximately 200 Tsembaga live. The mediation of the Tsembaga cosmology, which is symbolic of long-term sustainable relationships between system and environment, produces both *estar* and *bienestar* in Tsembaga society. Inadvertently, the Tsembaga do the right thing for the wrong reason. Anthony Wilden summarizes his analysis of the Tsembaga ritual cycle by observing, "With the exception of natural catastrophes or the coming of the white man, the Maring-Tsembaga system, co-evolved with nature, is quite capable of lasting to the end of time" (Wilden 1987a, 103). Analogously, Peggy Reeves Sanday, in *Female Power and Male Dominance* (1981), examines the 186 societies of the Standard Cross-Cultural Sample to underscore the fact that the technoscientific worldview, mediated by the Western Social Imaginary, is only one possible arrangement among many in terms of the relations between technics and culture.

An intriguing possibility, then, is the question of the escape from the Imaginary enframing or mediation of the present metaphysical *Ge-stell*. Heidegger refers to this possibility as the "Turning" (away from technological enframing) and discusses it in the essay of the same name. For Heidegger, the "Turning" is the unconcealment of that which has been concealed, namely the metaphysical mediation or enframing of the relation between humanity and the Real:

> the coming to presence of technology will be surmounted [*verwunden*] in a way that restores it into its yet concealed truth. . . . But the surmounting of a destining of Being—here and now the surmounting of Enframing—each time comes to pass out of the arrival of another destining that does not allow itself to be either logically or historically predicted or to be metaphysically construed as a sequence belonging to a process of history. (Heidegger 1977, 39)

Thus a "Turning" in social mediation would involve an "unconcealment" of the concealment of the Western Social Imaginary in the history of, in our case, Hispanic letters, and in particular the concealment of the role of technoscientific instrumental reason in Hispanic letters. Such a turning would come "out of the arrival of another destining" or social coding unpredictable and unconstructable from within Western metaphysics. Both Heidegger and Ortega assert this does not imply the archaic fallacy of a surmounting of technics through a return to a prelapsarian techno-innocence, but rather a surmounting of our relation with them through a new coding of the relationship between nature, society, and technics. In contrast to the symbolic sociocultural mediation described by Rappaport, Western scientific, cultural, and critical practices have sustained—through technics but not because of them—an Imaginary relation with the Real which has produced the present technological worldpicture.

In terms of cultural narrative, Hayden White speaks to the possible impact of the arrival of another destining or Social Coding unpredictable and unconstructable from within Western Metaphysics when he observes:

> to raise the question of the nature of narrative is to invite reflection on the very nature of culture and, possibly, even on the nature of humanity itself. . . . Far from being one code among many that a culture may utilize for endowing experience with meaning, narrative is a metacode, a human universal on the basis of which transcultural messages about the nature of a shared reality can be transmitted. (in Landow 1992, 103–4)

An important issue for present-day criticism, then, is the possibility of a future, or perhaps already present, "turning away." The above quote is taken from George P. Landow's now classic *Hypertext: The Convergence of Contemporary Critical Theory and Technology* (1992), a kind of prolegomena to a "becoming" turning away. The essential thrust of Landow's argument is that electronically mediated communication represents the realization of twentieth-century critical theory, the notion that theory has been made practice, a practice with unprecedented ramifications. Whereas Foucault (1979), Barthes (1971), and Derrida (1976) spoke in theoretical terms of the "death of the author," the "irreducible plurality of meaning" of the text, and denied the existence of an organizing center which furnishes structure and ultimate meaning, Landow asserts that what were formerly only theoretical constructs have now become reality in the hypertextual world of multimedial convergence known as the Web, the Net, virtual reality, and so forth.[5]

Another vertient of cybertheory goes a step beyond to suggest that not only human social discourse but also human material reality is changing. Katherine Hayles, in her influential article "Virtual Bodies and Flickering Signifiers," establishes two basic distinctions that separate what she, and many others, call the "posthuman" from everything that came before: the relation between human bodies and intelligent machines; and the form which signification takes:

> I understand "human" and "posthuman" to be historically specific constructions that emerge from different configurations of embodiment, technology,

and culture. . . . the posthuman implies a coupling so intense and multifac-
eted that it is no longer possible to distinguish meaningfully between the
biological organism and the informational circuits in which it is enmeshed.
Accompanying this change, I have argued, is a corresponding shift in how
signification is understood and corporeally experienced. In contrast to
Lacanian psycholinguistics, derived from the generative coupling of linguis-
tics and sexuality, flickering signification is the progeny of the fascinating
and troubling coupling of language and machine. (Hayles 1993, 111–12)

Hayles traces the evolution of writing from the humanist and realist "Book
and Author" stage, through an antihumanist and antirealist "Text and Author
Function" period, to the presently evolving posthuman and virtual reality phase
of the "Web Site," with its disembodied, fully distributed mode of cognition
(Hayles 1997). Hayles's point of view, echoed by many, sees the new narrative
form of the nonlinear, collaborative Web Site, with its model of decentered
and distributed cognition, in combination with the virtual worlds produced by
human-machine interfaces, as a possible "Turning," as the "arrival of another
destining that does not allow itself to be either logically or historically predicted or to be metaphysically construed as a sequence belonging to a process
of history" (Heidegger 1977, 39). Hayles asserts that:

For some time now there has been a rumor going around that the age of the
human has given way to the age of the posthuman. . . .Humans are not the
end of the line. Beyond them looms the cyborg, a hybrid species created by
crossing biological organism with cybernetic mechanism. (Hayles 1995, 321)

Roughly following Donna Haraway's position in *Simians, Cyborgs, and
Women* (1991), one popularized earlier by William Gibson in *Neuromancer*
(1984), those who champion the cyborg creed envisage a new *mestizaje* or
raza cósmica which will bridge the fourth and final discontinuity, that between human and machine.[6] According to Alejandro Piscitelli (1995), "it
deals with the arrival of the antonomastic *technological singularity*, that is,
the emergence of a post- and/or suprahuman intelligence and way of life"
(37). In other words, the cyborg represents a hybrid fusion of organism and
machine which offers a point of departure for a unique historical transformation, one beyond

the traditions of "Western" science and politics—the tradition of racist male-
dominated capitalism; the tradition of progress; the tradition of the appropriation of nature as resource for the productions of culture; the tradition of the
reproduction of the self from the reflection of the other. (Haraway 1991b, 150)

If changes in the material are to affect the social, they must effect changes in the Code. Hayles's second distinction, in which she proposes a new form of signification based on "the shift from presence and absence to pattern and randomness" (Hayles 1993, 80), her term is "flickering signifiers," addresses this issue. As cited above, according to Hayles, "flickering signification is the progeny of the fascinating and troubling coupling of language and machine" (112). The question, then, is does the electronically mediated information interface produce a new form of signification, a new narrative metacode, sufficiently radical to alter the present metaphysical *Ge-stell*? Piscitelli, arguing that indeed it does, makes the following points to support his position.

Taking a post-Saussurian stance, and using a variety of examples from Plato's attack on oral forms of communication to Sapir-Whorf, he first argues that "linguistic categories determine our perception and our understanding" (Piscitelli 1995, 135). He goes on to suggest that the new electronically mediated communicational categories will give rise to new and substantially different perceptions and understandings. If one accepts this hypothesis, then it is only necessary to demonstrate the radical differences of electronically mediated communication in order to show the inevitability of a new social narrative, pace Hayden White.

The differences in electronic discourse that Piscitelli highlights are the following: it is nonsequential and nonlinear; it does not refer to an origin or ultimate truth; cognition is decentered; it inverts the relation between metaphor and metonomy; it eliminates the traditional divide between the aesthetic and the anti or paraesthetic; it offers the possibility of transcending the written word altogether by means of iconic (graphics, video, sound, and so on) communication; and it breaks with physical and spacial constraints on identity, thus affording the possibility of multiple, if fragmented, identities (Piscitelli 1995, 135–57).

If the above observations sound like a laundry list of the attributes of postmodernism, it is because they are. As mentioned above, however, the important difference is that what were once theories are becoming, and in some cases have become, reality, a reality that has gone far beyond the theoretical imaginings of Barthes and Derrida. Although the fact that reality has outstripped theory is nothing new (indeed it is standard practice), it is nonetheless time for cultural criticism to devote itself seriously to the game of catchup. Mainstream Hispanic criticism has been markedly silent on the question of the new realities. While Hispanic writers have begun to enter these new spaces, and we can point to the hacker in Arturo Pérez-Reverte's *La piel del tambor*, the ill-fated use of compact disc Laura Esquivel's *La ley del amor*, the far better use of CD-ROM in Luis Goytisolo's *Mzungo*, the plethora of Spanish language e-zines, and a variety of didactic material available on-line and on CD-ROM as examples of this, leading edge cultural criticism in Latin America still considers hybridity more from the point of view of entering Modernity than leaving it.[7]

The importance of participating in both doing and thinking cyberculture cannot be overstated. Global relations are at a turning point, though whether it is the Turning or not is both logically and historically unpredictable. That will only be determined by what we do with the new possibilities, since "life is not fundamentally as so many centuries have believed it to be: contemplation, thought, theory. No; it is production, fabrication" (Ortega 1945–47b, 341–42).

I am not unaware that new technologies are routinely heralded as the solution to all problems, only to be co-opted shortly thereafter by the "system," nor am I blind to the present impossibility of reconciling cyberscience with Third World realities (Bastos and Cooper; Peña; Fortes and Adler Lomnitz), with its concomitant technological imperialism and dependency. Indeed, it is precisely for these reasons that the dominant discourse of the new communications systems needs be addressed in Latin America.

A cultural criticism which rejects the role of science and technology, and so jealously guards the "two cultures" distinction, is doomed to remain trapped within the enframing that produces the Imaginary oppositional social relations between discursive and nondiscursive practices, and between everyday practices and the institutionalization of these practices by theory, scientific and critical, both of which are, in the final analysis, messages in the discourse of the Social Imaginary. Only by a change in the enframing code can the messages of cultural and scientific practice be other than a replication of the present Social Imaginary and, as discussed above, new technics are an integral part of any possible recodification.

If we heed the "call" of both Heidegger and Ortega, we see that the present *Ge-stell* may be surmounted by a turning away from ratio-productive technologies and toward technics that sustain long-term sociocultural *bienestar*. A first step is to acknowledge the role of technics, in both Ortega and Heidegger's sense of the term, in the production of our sociocultural discourse, hardly an unreasonable request in the techno-productivist "age of information." Society must recognize in its relation with the institution of sociocultural criticism something that is its own product: the concealment of the relation between science, technology, and cultural studies by theoretical distancing. For this to be possible, Latin American cultural studies must overcome their institutional and imaginary denial. The one-dimensional Gramscian emphasis on counterhegemonic "discourses of resistance" with its attendant metaphysical inversionism still holds sway in the agonistic posture of most Latin American cultural studies vis-à-vis the demonic First World. Speaking of this false "postmodernism," Gianni Vattimo (1986), in *El fin de la modernidad*, observes:

> Thus—and examples can be found everywhere—the reaction to the devalorization of the supreme values, to the death of God, is the revindication—pathetic, metaphysical—of other, "truer" values (for example, the values of marginal cultures, of popular cultures, the opposite of the values of the dominant cultures; the destruction of literary and artistic canons, etc.). (28)

The archaic fallacy of a prelapsarian technoinnocence, of a magical realism, is as much a product of the metaphysical *Ge-stell* as is the global technoscientific culture it seeks to oppose. At issue should be not the existence of technology, but the uses of technology. The desire to surmount technology is the modern maneuver par excellence, while the desire to configure a nonmetaphysical system of necessities or *bienestar* in the face of the technological danger is the possible saving power.

If the role of technics is to reform nature according to a program of necessities, then their role can only change when this program of necessities, the collective definition of *bienestar*, is redefined. Two key features of any possible redefinition in a changing global context are message and code, that is, practice and theory, technics and *Ge-stell*. Only by changing mediation or message, or both, can the definition of *bienestar* be changed.

As the field of Hispanic cultural studies enters the twenty-first century, and inevitably moves to focus on the role of the technics and technology of, and through, the communications sciences, the imaginary nature of the division between science and the humanities will become ever more apparent, and so ever more difficult to deny. If one notion might serve as a point of departure for a reevaluation of science, technology, and culture, of code, context, and communication, perhaps it is that "the essence of technology is nothing technological." Those who fear to tread the technopath might well contemplate the possibility that where the technological danger is, grows the saving power also. In what follows, I wish to explore some of the technopaths that wend their way through Latin American narrative, in an effort to explore some of the ways in which Latin American narrative deals with "the skilful task of reconstructing the boundaries of daily life."

2

Constructing Technology in Latin American Literature

If the enframing discussed in the preceding chapter does indeed mediate our relation with each and every aspect of our experience, then we should also expect to find both scientific and technological discourse "setting upon" and "ordering" contemporary literary production, much as Nietzsche (1967) found the influence of Socratic Reason spreading through Greek tragedy. Thus one way to begin to look at the relation between science, technology, and literature is to consider the role of rational-productive discourse in enframing that which is "revealed" in literary discourse.

In *Myth and Archive* (1990), Roberto González Echevarría examines the notion of the mediating role of scientific discourse in the construction or ordering of Latin American literature and society. Focusing primarily on the authoritative discourse provided by the scientific travelers and travelogues of the eighteenth and nineteenth centuries, he argues that the narratives of scientific travelers such as Charles-Marie de la Condamine and Alexander von Humboldt decisively influenced many nineteenth-century writers, including such notables as Domingo Faustino Sarmiento and Andrés Bello. As the paradigmatic illustration of this influence, he points to the nature metaphor so prevalent in nineteenth-century Latin American literature and best exemplified in Bello's *Silvas americanas*.

González Echevarría also describes the mediating role of the human sciences in Latin American literature of the twentieth century. He asserts that after World War I and the concomitant fall from grace of positivism, the mediation of the natural sciences in Latin American literature is replaced by the mediation of the social sciences, primarily anthropology and ethnology. By way of illustration, he points to, among others, Lydia Cabrera (*El*

29

monte), who studied ethnology in Paris in the 1930s, Severo Sarduy (*De donde son los cantantes*), who was a student of French anthropologist Roger Bastide, and José María Arguedas (*Los ríos profundos*) and Miguel Barnet (*Biografía de un cimarrón*), who were both anthropologists (González Echevarría 1990, 14–15). An anthropologically mediated search for lost origins or "pasos perdidos," a place from which to begin afresh to build a new world, becomes a recurring theme in Latin American literature of this period.

Finally, in parallel with Foucault's prediction of the "end of man" that closes *The Order of Things* (Foucault 1973, 387), González Echevarría predicts that, given the recent *crisis de conscience* in the social sciences—James Clifford's term for the revelation of their literary nature (Clifford 1988, 22)—the social sciences will be replaced by the communication sciences as mediator of Latin American literature: "if one form of discourse appears to be acquiring hegemonic power it is that of communication systems" (González Echevarría 1990, 186). This suggests the possibility of a type of literary mediation that does not presuppose "Man" as the constituting subject of a world of objects, but rather locates humanity in a system of messages-in-circuit in an open-system/environment relation.

González Echevarría's reference to communication systems is therefore relevant in that it offers an alternative point of departure for the critical analysis of contemporary Latin American literature and culture which are, among many other things, communications systems. From this perspective, an essential aspect of any communication system is the coding that supplies the redundancy necessary to protect the message against the perturbations of a "noisy" environment (Shannon & Weaver 1964). All societal messages, including literary imagery, are products of the mediation of the ensemble of societal codes which constitute that society's Social Imaginary. Without this coding or redundancy, a given society must necessarily succumb to the effects predicted by the Second Law of Thermodynamics, that is, it would become more and more entropic over time, until it eventually dissolved into complete disorder. Thus the Social Imaginary is the key both to maintaining and to changing a given sociocultural system.

The notion of literary imagery as mediated messages leads to a related consideration, that of the images of scientists, science, and technology seen in contemporary Latin American fiction. These images reflect both past and present relations between society and technology in Latin America, and offer an insight into the possible futures of these relations. Because they are messages mediated by the Social Imaginary, these images offer a sense of how the popular imagination perceives itself in relation to the enframing and mediation of modern, ratio-productive technological worldviews. Furthermore, these images represent the range of negotiation available within the constraints of the Latin American Social Imaginary. Therefore, they are messages about both the boundaries and the "skilful task of reconstructing the boundaries of daily life" in Latin America, about order and possible transgression of that order, about how things are and how things might be.

While sharing many similarities with North American and European literary conceptualizations of technology, the images created in Latin American fiction also reflect the multiple sociohistoric prisms through which Latin American writers view the impact of technology. Additionally, in our present era, one can note a marked divergence between First and Third World literary criticism dealing with fictional representations of science and technology. Whereas in the nineteenth century writers on both sides of the Atlantic—from Zola, Balzac, Galdós and Dickens to Sarmiento, Euclides da Cunha and Anselmo Suárez y Romero—availed themselves of essentially the same positivist discourse of science through which to evaluate social relations, in the second half of the twentieth century there occurs a fork in the analytic path, a bifurcation between First and Third World perspectives.

Contemporary First World literature and literary criticism deal extensively and explicitly with scientific theory and technology. As evidence we have only to mention such writers as Philip K. Dick, Thomas Pynchon, Don Delillo, Neal Stephenson, and Kurt Vonnegut, and look at the ever growing body of literary criticism dealing both with science and technology in literature and with the application of scientific theory to literature—fractals, chaos theory, information and communication theory, strange attractors, cybernetics, complexity, undecidability, and so on.

Remarkably, with some notable exceptions, literary criticism within Latin America has sought to distance itself from the field of science and technology, a critical posture that has produced the erroneous impression that Latin American literature is little influenced by the discourses and the realities of science and technology. While some critics, mostly North Americans such as Jane Robinett, Floyd Merrell, Brian Conniff, and Thomas Weissert have dealt with the images of science and technology produced in Latin American literature, the tendency of mainstream criticism both in the First World and in Latin America to ignore this aspect of Latin American literature obscures an important side of contemporary Latin American culture, namely the attempt to negotiate a viable relation between science, technology, and society. Furthermore, an anachronistic insistence on maintaining the division between the "two cultures" of science and literature effectively yields the contested ground to those least likely to question the present technological enframing, namely the scientists, technocrats, and other prophets of technotopia. In fact, it is in the overlooked imagery of science, technology, and technics depicted in Latin American fiction that the enframing of Latin American Social Imaginary may be most usefully analyzed.

Contemporary Latin American narrative reveals a somewhat ambivalent but generally critical stance toward technology. The paradigmatic example of this attitude can be seen in the novel González Echevarría calls the archival Latin American novel, Gabriel García Márquez's *One Hundred Years of Solitude* (1967). The novel opens with the introduction of science and technology into Macondo through Melquíades and his array of technological inventions, from magnetized metal ingots to an entire alchemist's laboratory. As Lynn Thorndike (1923-77) has detailed, alchemy is a form of magic and represents a bridge between two forms of knowledge, magic and modern science. In *Dark Prisms: Occultism in Hispanic Drama* (1995), Robert Lima demonstrates that the interplay of natural and supernatural knowledge is a continuous theme in Hispanic letters. From the twelfth-century *Auto de los Reyes Magos*, through the *Celestina*, and up to the present day we see the interplay between "the human desire to know and connect with a supernatural order" (xi) and the attempt by science to regulate knowledge. It comes as no surprise, then, that a recurring theme in *One Hundred Years of Solitude* is the relation between technology and magic, natural and supernatural knowledge.

Throughout *One Hundred Years of Solitude*, which is a kind of historiography of scientific "progress" in Latin America, technology plays a key role: from José Arcadio Buendía, alchemist and so archetypical scientist, who draws up plans for solar warfare based on his experiments with a magnifying glass, to Aureliano Triste's "innocent yellow train" which initially brings only particular items of technology but eventually delivers the full-blown, rational-productive technological culture of Mr. Herbert and the banana company. As the exceptional North American critic and philosopher of technology Jane Robinett (1994) explains in her groundbreaking study *This Rough Magic: Technology in Latin American Fiction* (23-92, 189-214), the introduction of foreign technology results in a negative reorganization of social relations in Macondo. Where initially there existed Edenic bliss, successive technological interventions in this pristine reality destroy the environment (symbolized by the "enchanted region"), family structures, and ultimately Macondo itself, thanks to the banana company plague which eventually brings troops, massacres, and rain which lasts for four years, eleven months, and two days.

The banana company represents not just technology, but an entire techno-military-political structure which, as it plays out within the novel, demonstrates the end result of the rationalization of the world, or what Theodor Adorno and Max Horkheimer called the dialectic of enlightenment. The catastrophe brought on by the full-blown technological constellation of the banana company, a metaphor for the concept of reality optimized by rational design, provides a striking example of what Gianni Vattimo, in his study of the final stages of Modernity, has characterized, without specifically addressing the novel in question, as the counter-finality of reason:

> the rationalization of the world turns against reason and its ends of perfection and emancipation, and does so not by error, accident or a chance distortion, but precisely to the extent that it is more and more perfectly accomplished. (Vattimo 1968, 78)

The vision of technology in *One Hundred Years of Solitude* is a dark one, then, as the setting upon and ordering for use of everything in Macondo eventually brings about total cataclysm.

Within the novel, in marked contrast to the techno-productivist image of the banana company, García Márquez offers an alternative conceptualization of possible system-environment relations. At one level, this alternative view can be described simply as magic, and indeed, instances of the supernatural appear regularly in *One Hundred Years of Solitude*: ghosts, clairvoyance, levitations, resurrections, telepathy, indelible crosses of ashes, a rain of tiny yellow flowers, the astonishing fecundity of certain animals, enchanted regions, a nearly five-year rain, and a cataclysmic windstorm, to mention but a few.

Yet at another level, as Robinett suggests (96), the magical elements in *One Hundred Years of Solitude* can be construed as a call for a new relationship between society and nature. That the present techno-productivist system of infinite growth must sooner or later self-destruct, given the finite limits of natural and human resources, appears undeniable. Thus alternative approaches are essential, and the magic in *One Hundred Years of Solitude* provides one such alternative conceptualization, for it represents not rational utility, efficiency, and maximization of productivity and profit, but rather the possibility of a co-evolved, long-term sustainable relation with humankind's organic and inorganic environment. The images of magic in *One Hundred Years of Solitude* are messages mediated by a different type of *Ge-stell*, a "Social Symbolic" rather than a "Social Imaginary."

As mentioned above, the term *Social Symbolic* refers to a social mediation that represents (indirectly) other values. An example can be found in the case of the Montagnais-Laskapi of the Labrador plateau whose use of divination by burnt animal bones in their hunts produces a random hunting pattern which serves to prevent the depletion of a vital resource (Moore 1969). The "illogical" magic of divination ensures the long-term survival of both predator and prey, something that does not happen under ratio-productive "optimization" of natural resource harvesting. Co-evolved symbolic mediation between system and environment accomplishes the right thing for the (apparently) wrong reason.

In the case of García Márquez's novel, the natural magic which ultimately destroys the rationalist project of the banana company symbolizes the negative feedback loops necessary to the establishment of a symbiotic relationship between society and nature. The magic in *One Hundred Years of Solitude* reminds us that humanity is dependent on nature, and not the other way around. It reminds us, in the words of Gregory Bateson (1989), that "The system which destroys its environment ultimately destroys itself" (493).

In Isabel Allende's *The House of the Spirits* (1982), which opens in "the heart of the twentieth century, this century of light, science, and technology," the foreign black magic of technology is in league with the military-political forces of evil. Mr. Herbert of *One Hundred Years of Solitude* is now the "tiny gringo" expert Mr. Brown and the banana plague is now the plague of ants at the estate of Tres Marías. Mr. Brown's foreign technology is pitted against the local knowledge of Pedro Segundo García, the estate's foreman. At this level, local knowledge or "magic" wins out but, as in *One Hundred Years of Solitude*, the novel ends in an apocalyptic event, the coup d'état in which military technology and foreign experts replace Allende with Pinochet.

The case of Pedro Segundo García illustrates the contrast between worldviews mediated by the Social Imaginary and those mediated by the Social Symbolic. Mr. Brown, an expert not on insects but on insecticides, represents uses of technology for the purpose of death and domination, a competitive worldview which sees both nature and humanity as opponents to be conquered in a Darwinian struggle for survival. By contrast, as Robinett (1994) points out:

Pedro García's magic, which also includes its techniques, is directed not at destroying, but at restoring a balance between living things. It mediates between life forms and fosters life in order to resolve problems, rather than resorting to the disruption of reproductive cycles and the wholesale slaughter of (female) life forms. (116)

In general terms, these two novels indicate that contemporary Latin American fiction, in contrast to an earlier view which saw technology as the solution rather than the problem, tends toward a somewhat Faustian response. Technology is characterized as imposed foreign domination, a deal made with the First World devil that grants temporary power to the few, but that ultimately proves ill-suited to local realities and leads inevitably to disastrous consequences. Here, the post hoc or, perhaps better, post Enlightenment rationalization of domination, reason, has, as Max Weber predicted, turned from controlling nature to controlling humanity.

In both novels, technology is contrasted with or, for Robinett, opposed to magic, which represents a mysterious supplement beyond rational control, an area inhabited by concepts such as intuition, emotion, and the spiritual, and peopled by those marginalized groups who are on the receiving end of technological domination, that is, nature, women, indigenous groups, and so forth. The alternative epistemologies offered in these novels suggest that these concepts and groups defined as outside the space of rational productivity are the environment of reason and technoscience, and so the ground of their very Being. The relation between those groups and concepts defined as constituent parts of rational technoculture and those defined as contradictory to and incompatible with the rational project is not one of opposition, but rather one of system and environment. To place the two realms in a relation of opposition that demonizes technology is to misrecognize the nature of the relationship. Alongside the social construction of nature there exists the material reality of nature. The relations between society and nature are mediated by both these factors. As these novels indicate, when these two mediational influences present contradictory worldviews, disaster eventually ensues. When social evolution or succession toward a symbiotic relation with nature is blocked by a competitive *Ge-stell* that places society and nature in an either/or relation of binary opposition, the only two remaining possibilities are revolution or extinction.

Not all Latin American writers, however, insist that the monster created by science and technology must destroy the doctor's castle. Following Robinett (1994, 153–88), we may observe that in *Gabriela, Clove and Cinnamon* (1958), the Brazilian Jorge Amado offers a somewhat different view of the mix of man and woman, magic and science. In *Gabriela* Amado suggests that *"Ordem e Progresso!"* (Order and Progress!), the motto on the Brazilian flag, may well be achieved through technology. Indeed, the novel deals with the changes that occur as new technologies replace old ones in the transition from a closed, oligarchic society ruled by semifeudal plantation owners to an open, modern, entrepreneurial society. The engineers who remove the sandbar blocking the port of Ilhéus reshape not only nature but also local society, politics, and culture.[1] The old *caudillo* Ramiro Bastos, patriarch and strongman of the region, is replaced by the civilized ways of Mundinho Falcâo, the rich, educated, and thoroughly modern-thinking newcomer from the big city, thanks to the power of imported technology. Unfortunately, although Falcâo represents a step toward democracy, it is a small step and very few are actually empowered because political relations still remain trapped within a competitive context. The new technocrats replace the old *caudillos*, but the underlying oppositional and competitive nature of the power structure remains unchanged. At the political level, then, the difference between technologies of domination and technologies of empowerment is still problematic due to the either/or enframing of a positivist and analytical social context.

In contrast to the politicians, the title character Gabriela, a young, innocent, and beautiful economic refugee recently arrived from the impoverished North, views technology not as means to dominate both nature and humanity, but rather as a means to redefine and then realize personal and social well-being, an attitude reminiscent of José Ortega y Gasset's insistence that *bienestar* or well-being is the true human necessity and ought to be the goal of technology. Gabriela's primary expertise, bordering on the magical, is culinary, but her influence also extends to other areas of *bienestar*. Her technical skill in cooking provides her with a power base from which to change local political, social, and moral dogma. By using her power to successfully challenge and overturn basic social codes, specifically the "code of honor" which requires a man to kill an unfaithful wife, Gabriela effects change not only at the message level, but also at the level of the code. As Robinett (1994) explains (182–85), the message is clear: technological expertise and knowledge is a power capable of liberation as well as domination. Nevertheless, Gabriela still represents the prelapsarian innocence of Edenic nature, with "the soul of a child" (372) but capable of "nights of magic. . . of elemental forces released in bed . . . with Gabriela consuming herself as in a flame" (333). In *Gabriela*, Amado appears to suggest the need for Symbolic mediation, in spite of his inability to avoid the metaphysical nature/culture binaries of an Edenic archaism.

In all of the novels discussed here we find versions of the obligatory fall from grace after disobeying the divine mandate not to eat of the Tree of (technoscientific) Knowledge. All three suggest, to varying degrees, the recovery of an original state of innocence and plenty through a return to "nature." Nature is seen as a composite construction comprised of those elements defined as technoculture's other: woman, intuition, emotion, magic, indigenous knowledge, innocence, and so forth. Where the novels differ is in their assessment of the role of mediation in effecting long-term sustainable relationships between society and its environment. This reflects the ambiguous history of the relation between society, technology, and nature in the Western Imaginary.

The image of nature as Edenic cornucopia has long served as the justification for technological intervention in everything from irrigation projects designed to "make the desert bloom" to the genetic engineering programs of the new biotechnologies. The unquestioned value of abundance has linked ever-increasing production, and hence technology, with the common good. Analogously, political theories from capitalism to Marxism have linked material abundance with freedom. The solution to social conflict is seen as simply supplying everyone with enough material goods to make them happy. The image of the abundance of an enchanted Eden, far from being antitechnological, represents precisely that view of *bienestar* that drives technological "progress," and so participates fully in the Western *Ge-stell*.

At the same time, the theme of a return to Eden has also evoked images of a pure, innocent, and organic relationship between society and nature, of a time before the fall from grace. This archaic and apocalyptic view seeks to retrieve an "authentic" relation between humanity and nature, one unmediated by the dialectic of enlightenment and its subsequent capitalist, imperialist, and ecological exploitations of humanity and the natural world. Apart from the fact that this view gives rise to right-wing, fundamentalist programs for the restoration of traditional culture, or liberal utopian criticism of technoscientific civilization, the main problem with this view is that it too remains trapped within Western binary metaphysics. This view simply reverses the myth of progress into a myth of origins, and idealizing a time of Edenic perfection is as fallacious as idealizing the future, which is what the ideal of progress does. Above all, these binary approaches obscure the role of social mediation in determining the uses of technology.

Returning to *Gabriela*, we find a variant of the two standard Edenic stories. In Amado's account, a new Eden is constructed through an alliance between nature and technology, an alliance mediated by the same constellation of elements which comprise nature in the first type of Edenic narrative. Woman, magic, intuition, and so on mediate the relation between technology and nature in such a manner as to place human beings in a symbiotic relationship with both nature and technology. While it appears questionable to assign gender to mediational alternative technological development strategies, as Amado seems to do in *Gabriela*, the concept of mediation is indeed the key to understanding the essence of technology which is, as Heidegger reminds us, nothing technological. In *Gabriela*, Amado makes the important point that technology can be usefully contested only at the level of the code, the mediation or enframing that is the essence of technology. To effect other than simply cosmetic or esthetic changes in the game, one must change the rules, not the players. While Falcâo's use of technology merely changes the players, Gabriela's contribution to Illéhusian society is to change the rules, a harbinger of the promise offered by the changing roles of women in present day Latin America, as seen in the multiclass and multiethnic coalitions formed by Latin American women in an effort to change social, political, and economic patterns in Latin America.

Technology does not lead inevitably to authoritarian states and ecological disaster. All human societies employ technology, and many develop co-evolved, long-term sustainable relationships with their environments. The deciding factor is the social construction of a given society's definition of a desirable standard of living or *bienestar* in Ortega's sense of the term. As discussed in the previous chapter, according to Ortega (1945–47b) in "Meditación de la técnica":

> That which Man calls living, living well or well-being, is a fluid term, infinitely variable. And because the repertoire of human necessities is directly linked to the definition of well-being, these too are infinitely variable. Finally, given that technics are the repertoire of acts motivated or caused by, and inspired in this system of necessities, they too constitute a proteiform reality, in constant mutation. (330)

The fact that a given society's "system of necessities" is constrained and mediated by the Social Imaginary raises the question of the possible influence of literature in reshaping that Social Imaginary. If a given society's "system of necessities" is indeed in constant mutation, then the mutual interface between the discourses of technology and cultural creativity would seem to be an apt arena for reconfiguring the present Social Imaginary, and with it the current "system of necessities" and the concomitant technologies employed to realize those "necessities."

The discourse of magic portrayed in these novels reflects the trend in interdisciplinary thinking which does in fact emphasize the need for local solutions and appropriate technologies in order to reduce Latin American technological dependency and so reduce both endocolonialism and domination by transnational corporations. This raises the question of the possibility of developing an alternative to the Social Imaginary, a Social Symbolic capable of contesting the global communicational imaginary, the ideological global apparatuses. In the final analysis, the issue revolves not around the question of appropriate technologies, but rather around the question of appropriate Imaginaries or, better yet, appropriate Social Symbolics.

The novels discussed here, and many others, offer multiple images of technology based on the perceived relations between technology and society in Latin America. The field of literature is one of the public forums in which these competing visions are debated, and in which solutions are suggested. This debate has profound implications for the future of all concerned, especially in light of the current impossibility of developing a critical scientific mass in Latin America (as documented in Fortes and Adler Lomnitz), and hence the inevitability of continued technological dependency. The question is, will this dependency be on technologies of domination or technologies of empowerment? This question will be decided in the debate over appropriate social mediations. By positioning itself within the activities of science and technology, literary theory can cease to be an uninformed victim and become an informed and active participant in the decisions that determine our collective future, that is, in "the skilful task of reconstructing the boundaries of daily life." If society is to evolve a symbolic mediation and so also a cooperative rather than a competitive relation with its environment, literature and literary theory must somehow find the middle way between the superstition from which science liberated humanity and the discovery of the counter-finality of reason, the sad fact that the rationalization of the world has turned against reason and its ends of perfection and emancipation. Literature must somehow, while demythologizing the myth of reason, not return to an earlier naive relation with myth. In Nietzsche's words, it must "continue to dream knowing that it is dreaming" (Nietzsche 1974, 116). I would suggest that it behooves us to participate in this ongoing discussion, since it cannot but directly affect each and every one of us.

3

The Technological Other

In *Becoming a Scientist in Mexico: The Challenge of Creating a Scientific Community in an Underdeveloped Country* (1994), Jacqueline Fortes and Larissa Adler Lomnitz paint a rather gloomy picture of the possibility of developing a "critical scientific mass" in Mexico or, indeed, in any Latin American country. The specific reasons given are many, but essentially the problem revolves around a negative cultural perception of the scientific ethos, since "science did not result from internal development; it is an imported cultural product" (161). This view is echoed in a whole host of recent studies (Hernández-Boada 1995; Martine 1985; Sutz 1993). The consensus seems to be that the most Latin America can aspire to in terms of research science is the construction of local appropriate technologies, and even these are suspect (Peña 1992).[1] Thus, in spite of a few isolated success stories such as Cuba's Center for Genetic Engineering and Biotechnology, from the perspective of the scientific community Latin America's continued scientific and technological dependence, and hence continued vulnerability to exploitation by transnationals and others, would appear to be a foregone conclusion.

If this is indeed the case, it does not bode well for those Latin Americans who would prefer to mold their own futures. If we accept that technology plays an ever-increasing role in shaping our lives, then it follows that to lose control over both the production of technology and technological production is to lose control over nearly all areas of human relations, from work and leisure to society, politics, and culture. The question concerning who controls technology is central to determining who we are. One must ask, then, apart from the scientific literature, where else does society forge its relation to technology, and why is this question not central to cultural studies?

Regarding the second part of the above question, a partial explanation for the relative lack of interest in technology shown by cultural studies, apart from the traditional rift between the "two cultures," appears to lie in the transparency of technology. This very book will be written, spell-checked, e-mailed, printed, and distributed by technological means, all from the controlled (climate and otherwise) environment of my office. But unless something malfunctions, I will be oblivious to the technology which surrounds me, it has become "second nature" to me. Indeed, so pervasive is the influence of technology that there are those, Jean Baudrillard (1983) among them, who would have it that first nature no longer exists, that we now inhabit a world of simulacra and will soon occupy the virtual reality of cyberspace.[2]

Once this transparency is recognized, the extent of the sociocultural impact of technology begins to acquire a sharper focus. One area of culture in which the "is" and the "ought" of technosocial relations is reviewed and debated is the field of literature. As we have seen, Latin American literature has a longstanding relationship with the discourses of science and technology, from the nineteenth-century influences of positivism and the natural sciences, through the early twentieth century preoccupation with the social sciences, especially anthropology and ethnography, and on to such contemporary narratives as Gabriel García Márquez's *One Hundred Years of Solitude* (1971), Isabel Allende's *The House of the Spirits* (1986), and Laura Esquivel's *Like Water for Chocolate: A Novel of Monthly Installments with Recipes, Loves, and Home Remedies* (1990).[3] One public forum, then, in which to express an awareness of and a reaction to the evergrowing control exerted by technology is provided by literature (and cinema), a forum in which popular beliefs can be symbolized and constructed, and the dominant discourse of science contested.

From this, at least two questions follow: what are the popular beliefs expressed in narrative (including film), and what do they portend for future relations between science, technology, and society? Clearly, it is beyond the scope of this chapter to consider these questions from a broad enough perspective to account for all the varying takes on technology represented in even the few novels mentioned above. Therefore, in what follows I wish to concentrate on one issue, the depiction of the technological Other, the gringo scientist, in *Like Water for Chocolate*.[4] The recurrent motif of the gringo scientist represents one strand in the sociocultural process of weaving popular attitudes toward foreign technology in developing countries, and so participates in both mirroring and constructing popular sentiment toward technology in Latin America. The novel and the subsequent film are worthy of examination inasmuch as they have enjoyed wide distribution both in Spanish and in translation, and so can reasonably be assumed to have substantially influenced popular opinion.

In *Like Water for Chocolate*, we first see the gringo scientist Doctor John Brown when he arrives to care for Rosaura. Dr. Brown is a medical doctor, and has been summoned from his home in Eagle Pass, Texas, to assist in the delivery of Rosaura and Pedro's first child, later named Roberto. Because Rosaura's husband Pedro, who is sent to fetch the doctor, is detained by government troops, Dr. Brown does not arrive in time and the novel's protagonist Tita finds herself alone with her sister Rosaura at the crucial moment. Suddenly aware of her own lack of knowledge in these matters, she curses her schoolteachers and her mother alike for not having prepared her for the task of delivery, and calls upon the former household cook and wetnurse to Tita, the now deceased Nacha for help (78). In what would appear to be a manifestation of the supernatural, Nacha hears her prayers and comes to her aid: "Then, following the instructions that Nacha whispered in her ear, she knew perfectly well all the steps she had to follow: cut the umbilical cord at a precise place and time . . ." (79). When Doctor Brown arrives the following day, the true extent of the miracle is scientifically confirmed, right down to the Latinate technical terminology: "According to the Doctor, Rosaura suffered an attack of eclampsia that could have killed her. He was quite surprised at the way in which Tita had attended to her with such skill and decision under such difficult circumstances" (80).

That a gringo doctor is sent for, indeed he is the family physician, rather than a Mexican obstetrician, indicates the prestige enjoyed by North American science and scientists and the lack of faith in local practitioners in Mexico. This reflects the contemporary view of medicine in Mexico, where nearly everyone who can afford it travels to the United States for medical care, and the local government-sponsored program of medical care, *Seguro Social*, is considered suspect at best. In the realm of medical technoscientific knowledge, then, it would appear that Mexican popular opinion cedes the field to North American expertise.

However, Tita's success, which is due not to knowledge she received from the government-sponsored school system or from her mother, but rather from the scientifically inexplicable manifestation of Nacha, appears to contest the view that privileges foreign science and technology over local knowledge or traditional folkways and home remedies (the *remedios caseros* of the title). The school system can be read as a metaphor of the foreign (French) positivist science of the *Porfiriato* period immediately preceding the Revolution, while her mother is effectively a symbol of patriarchal participation in the dominant, rational, epistemological discourse, inasmuch as she sent for Brown in the first place, and consistently refuses to accept supernatural explanations for anything until the final moments of the novel, when she herself ironically becomes a supernatural apparition. In contrast, Nacha represents nature, emotion, intuition, artesanal technics such as cooking, local or indigenous knowledge, and the cryptic "many other things" (14). The implication is that Nacha, who is either *mestiza* or *india*, has access to another, more authentic type of knowledge, an "original" knowledge that was once known to all of humanity, but which has since been lost in the "fall" into scientific knowledge and the concomitant rush to construct our modern technoscientific worldview.

As González Echevarría has pointed out in *Myth and Archive* (1990), the privileging of mythical knowledge is characteristic of Latin American narrative in the first half of the twentieth century, beginning in the period following World War I, when this type of originary knowledge was seen as a point of departure from which to begin again to reconstruct a world shattered by war on a global scale. In this era of the Decline of the West and the demise of positivism, Latin American literature took on an anthropological mediation.[5] The mediation of the discourse of structural anthropology, ethnography, and certain artistic avant-garde movements such as surrealism produced a generally apocalyptic view that placed Western technoscientific culture in opposition to an "authentic" relation with ourselves and with nature, and viewed it as part and parcel of colonialism, imperialism, and capitalist exploitation.

As discussed in the previous chapter, in the case of the anthropologically mediated novels González Echevarría refers to, such as Miguel Angel Asturias's *Leyendas de Guatemala*, Alejo Carpentier's *Los pasos perdidos*, and José María Arguedas's *Los ríos profundos*, this turn in Latin American literature was in reaction to the failure of the previous mediation provided by the hegemonic discourse of the natural sciences, which followed the model of the scientific travelers and travelogues of the eighteenth and nineteenth centuries, among them Alexander von Humboldt, Charles-Marie de la Condamine, and Charles Darwin. Examples of the influence of these scientific travelers and travelogues include such novels as Domingo Faustino Sarmiento's *Facundo*, Anselmo Suárez y Romero's *Francisco*, and Euclides da Cunha's *Os Sertôes*. In these positivist novels the uniqueness of the

New World is reported and then interpreted by a scientific observer whose objective "method" qualifies him to read nature and so reveal its truth.

However, in the case of *Like Water for Chocolate*, although the novel is set during the period of the Mexican Revolution with all its accompanying destruction and hence proof of the counter-finality of the positivist project in Mexico, it was written in the late 1980s, a period of hegemony not of the natural sciences but rather of the communications sciences. Therefore, one must ask, is the appropriation of anthropological discourse as a discourse of resistance fitting or anachronistic; is it, in the words of Claudine Potvin, "postmodern parody or simply cliché?"[6] One might argue that from within the historical context of the novel it is eminently appropriate, but if we are considering the question from within the context of the construction of contemporary popular opinion vis-à-vis the relations between society and technology in Latin America, it would appear that contrasting timeless local or indigenous knowledge with a dated positivist scientific paradigm might well be an exercise in futility. In the intervening period, anthropological mediation itself has suffered a *crise de conscience* involving the revelation of its literary nature (Clifford 1988, 22), and this has created a subsequent metadiscourse within the social sciences and within Latin American narrative (*Rayuela, Yo el supremo*).[7] Also, in the final decades of the twentieth century the unveiling of the social roots of the supposedly "value-free" natural sciences has produced a crisis and a new metadiscourse within this field also.[8] Finally, the objective scientific observer of positivism has given way to the anonymous technocrat of the panoptic communicational apparatus. Given these developments, the question must necessarily arise, has Esquivel simply resuscitated the discourses of anthropology and positivism for one more flogging, or is there another way to interpret the relation between Tita, the gringo scientist, and Rosaura's childbirth?

In *Imperial Leather: Race, Gender, and Sexuality in the Colonial Contest* (1995), Anne McClintock devotes considerable effort to demonstrating the relation between imperialism, colonization, and the image of the female body. Discussing Jan van der Straet's famous drawing (ca. 1575) of the "discovery" of America, in which "A fully armored Vespucci stands erect and masterful before a naked and erotically inviting woman, who inclines toward him from a hammock" (25-26), McClintock argues that the female figure—America—represents "nature's invitation to conquest . . . while Vespucci confronts the virgin land with the patrimony of scientific mastery and imperial might. . . . and stakes male Europe's territorial rights to her body and, by extension, the fruits of her land" (26). Relatedly, Paula

A Treichler (1990), in "Feminism, Medicine, and the Meaning of Child-birth," discusses the birth of "modern obstetrics" in the nineteenth century and the concomitant control over childbirth achieved and since maintained by the dominant technoscientific medical culture. For Treichler, the defini-tion of childbirth as a medical event, "a potentially diseased condition that *routinely* requires the arts of medicine to overcome the processes of na-ture" (119, italics in original) opens the door to male, scientific, imperial control of the female body. From the point of view of medical science, the body is seen as a production factory, "with physicians the technicians who keep it running efficiently and profitably" (121). Treichler goes on to re-view some of the voices that have arisen from within feminism to contest this domination, concluding with that of the novelist Margaret Atwood who, in *Surfacing*, equates medicalized childbirth with U.S. imperialism. The model developed by McClintock and Treichler demonstrates the gendered nature of the phenomenon described by Max Weber whereby the post hoc rationalization of domination, reason, turns from controlling nature to con-trolling humanity.

Can we then suggest as a possible reading of Tita's performance in Rosaura's childbirth that of an anti-imperialist, anticolonialist analogy of the relations of colonizing gringo scientist and colonized woman/Nature? Does Tita's success represent a discourse of resistance in opposition to colonizing gringo science? At first glance, the answer might well be in the affirmative, for clearly the discourse of techno-imperialism has been a gendered discourse of power in which that defined as female has been ap-propriated and even victimized. However, if the parable of Tita's success-ful rejection of foreign science and technology is to provide a useful contribution to the construction of a successful alternative relation to tech-nology in Latin America, it must be based upon a viable worldview and not complicit in reproducing the idealization and manipulation of "the (super)natural."

Rosaura's childbirth is not completely natural; rather, it requires inter-vention. This successful intervention is based on another knowledge sys-tem, one not susceptible to rational demonstration, which, in the novel, proves itself at least as effective as technoscience. Thus, in pragmatic terms the two systems are equally effective, while local or indigenous knowledge has the added benefit of escaping from the exploitative imperial control of modern medical science and the male, imperial, domination of instrumen-tal reason. But Tita's success rests on the slippery slope of Nacha's more "authentic" mythical knowledge. It is therefore necessary to consider some of the other factors involved in the construction of Nacha's knowledge.

Many recent social studies of science have demonstrated the constructed nature of modern scientific discourse (Latour and Woolgar 1979; Bleier 1984; Harding 1986; Haraway 1991a; Rose 1993; Wood 1992). These studies have recognized that supposedly objective science and its method are in fact textual constructs of society, in much the same way as literature, history, and politics are products of their social milieu, and so subject to the same biases and constraints as any other social commodity. On this view, the scientific worldview that was supposed to emancipate humanity from myth and superstition turns out to be a mythical construct itself. Gianni Vattimo (1992) summarizes these developments as follows:

> Consequently, the idea that the course of history could be thought of as enlightenment, as the liberation of reason from the shadows of mythical knowledge, has lost its legitimacy. Demythologization has itself come to be seen as myth. (39)

But even if we fully accept this strong program in the sociology of scientific knowledge, does it follow that the previous myths are suddenly relegitimized? If, as Nietzsche (1986) pointed out, all truth is "error" inasmuch as it is founded on the relative exigencies of our social context and not on transcendent values (if God is dead), are there no criteria for choosing provisional values? In the case of the construction of popular opinion regarding technology in Latin America, I would argue that those values are most useful which promote the long-term survival and well-being of the individuals and societies impacted by technology. In order to determine whether or not Nacha's alternative epistemology offers a viable antidote to the foreign, male, rational technoscience represented by the gringo scientist in *Like Water for Chocolate*, we need first elucidate other aspects of the alternative worldview constructed in the novel.

During Brown's evaluation of Tita's expertise in the delivery of Rosaura's child, the doctor notices a curious and alien perception insinuating itself into his body even as he concentrates on his rational appraisal of the medical situation: "a strange sensation ran through his body, awakening and activating his dormant feelings" (80). What is happening, of course, is that the emotions of the cold, rational man of science have been awakened by the presence of Tita.

In fact, a *leitmotif* of the novel is Tita's ability to elicit emotional responses in others. This mystical power is revealed in many ways, including the effect she has on Brown and Pedro, but primarily in her cooking. Her

culinary creations are works of art that illicit uniform emotional responses
in those who taste the food she prepares. These responses are a direct reflection of Tita's emotional state at the time she prepares the meals. There
is often a cause and effect relation between Tita's emotional state during
the food preparation, certain of her bodily fluids which serve as vectors,
and the emotional response engendered in the receptors of her culinary
messages. If, for example, her tears fall in the food during preparation, the
meal produces a melancholy response, while if her blood is introduced, an
aphrodisiac effect ensues, and so on. Thus, mind and body are linked
alchemically, in contrast to the prevailing ratio-scientific mind/body dual-
ism. Since Tita was taught to cook by Nacha (in fact she was practically
raised by Nacha in the kitchen), Tita's cooking can be construed as an extension of an indigenous artesanal tradition, as part of the traditional knowledge and techniques of a timeless society in which mind and body were
never separated, in which emotion was never subordinated to reason.

In the novel, this more authentic form of knowledge, represented by
Tita/Nacha/Luz del amanecer's prehispanic culinary technique, is contrasted
with North American cooking, and hence by analogy with the distortions
and the sensual and emotional impoverishment of technoscientific civilization. When Tita finally rebels against her mother, the tyrannical Mamá Elena,
she suffers an emotional trauma and is pronounced insane by Mamá Elena,
who orders Dr. Brown to commit Tita to an asylum. Brown instead brings
her to his home in Texas, where she eventually recovers. When she first
arrives, her meals are prepared and brought to her by Caty, "a 70 year old
North American lady" (114). But in spite of her vital need for sustenance at
this critical juncture in her recovery, she finds the North American food so
banal and tasteless as to be inedible: "at times Tita didn't even taste the
food, it was insipid and totally disagreeable to her" (114). The food of the
culture of reason is so lacking in the spice of emotion that Tita prefers
death to culinary dishonor. Indeed, throughout the novel the representatives of masculine, ratio/military repression—Mamá Elena, Sergeant
Treviño, Gertrudis, Caty—are shown to be incompetent in the emotional
art of cooking, thus reinforcing the artist/scientist binary.

Fortunately, before a fate worse than everything short of eating North
American cuisine can overtake her, Tita catches a whiff of smoke coming
from the margins of Brown's technoscientific complex and she is saved,
transported back to an earlier, more authentic time:

> It was coming from a small room at the back of the patio. It was an odor so
> pleasant and familiar that it made her open the window in order to inhale it

more deeply. With her eyes closed, she could see herself seated next to Nacha on the kitchen floor making corn tortillas; she could see the pot where an aromatic stew was brewing, and next to it the beans were starting to boil . . . without hesitation she decided to go find out who was cooking. It couldn't be Caty. Whoever was producing this type of culinary perfume definitely knew how to cook. (115)

The cook, "very similar to Nacha," turns out to be Brown's grandmother, whose amerindian name translates to Spanish as Luz del amanecer [Light of Dawn]. She is a Native American, possibly of the tribe known as the Kickapoo in English-speaking North America, who was abducted by Brown's grandfather and subsequently married to him, much to the dismay of his family. Luz was ostracized by the family and relegated to a small room at the edge of the gringo social space, where she happily continued her nonscientific investigations into the curative properties of local plants. Luz's indigenous cooking knowledge saves Tita's life, and so demonstrates the superiority of her more authentic worldview. Because Luz is also a curandera, a connection is established between the curative powers of indigenous cooking and these same curative powers, and hence superiority, of holistic, indigenous approaches to the areas considered the preserve of Western science, such as botany, biology and medicine. Thus, the critique of Western rationality passes from the artistic arena to the scientific.

Constructing a parallel with recent scientific admissions of the medicinal values of indigenous, herbal, healing techniques, the narrator speaks of "the huge difference of opinions and concepts that existed between these representatives of two cultures [science and literature?] so very different" (116). Thus we learn that it is only with the failure of "the best scientific knowledge" to save the life of Brown's greatgrandfather that the family is forced to recognize the wisdom of "la kikapú" in the dramatic moment in which she steps in and saves his life, "singing strange melodies to him while placing herbal poultices on him in the midst of the smoke from the incense and copal" (117). In microcosm, we witness the simultaneous destruction of one myth concerning control over nature and its replacement with another: "from that day on, `the Kickapoo' became the family doctor, and was fully recognized as a miracle worker by the North American community" (118).

John Brown's scientific career also reflects the evolution of Western science with respect to indigenous knowledge. Much as modern science began with alchemy, broke with it to legitimize itself through rational method, and has recently returned to examine non-Western science through the lens of method, John spends his youth at Luz's side in the "small laboratory," goes to the university where he learns to repudiate "primitive" superstition, "modern theories . . . were in enormous contradiction with those of his grandmother" (118), and finally returns home to "prove scientifically all the miraculous cures performed by 'Light of Dawn'" (118). But even as he accepts the efficacy of Luz's practices, he maintains his rational, objective approach to medicine, "it was with no problem whatsoever that he disassociated his mental activity from his physical activity" (118). He remains in a world in which mind and body are separated. He still doesn't get it, and his failure to understand the nonrational costs him his chance for true happiness, defined as emotional fulfillment with Tita. Thus, even as gringo rationality attempts to approach its "opposite"—emotion—the effort is doomed from the start due to the rational context in which reason must necessarily operate. The two cultures are inevitably mutually exclusive and, much as Caty cannot duplicate Luz's cooking, John and Western science can neither comprehend nor equal Luz's knowledge of nature.

The theme of incomplete, gringo reason versus holistic, indigenous emotion is also illustrated through the relations between Tita, John, and Pedro. Throughout the novel Tita has been forced to sublimate her emotions due to the repression of the patriarchal Mamá Elena, who forbids her to marry Pedro in order that Tita might care for her in her old age. Pedro has a chance to seize the emotional day, to let passion rule and change the course of history, but he fails because he cannot bring himself to challenge the established rational order: "If Pedro had asked Tita to run away with him, she wouldn't have thought twice, but he didn't do it" (60). Instead, he makes the more "reasonable" move of marrying Rosaura in order to be close to Tita. Thus, the one rational decision that Pedro makes in the entire novel costs him his chance for emotional fulfillment.

After John saves Tita by curing her hysteria, a "female" mental illness, she feels indebted to him and so agrees to marry him. Besides, she calculates that life with John will bring her a sort of measured serenity, a cool happiness, and so the marriage seems quite logical and reasonable. However, in the end she cannot surrender to the voice of reason and the heat of passion carries the day: "Pedro tenderly rubbed his cheek across Tita's, and she felt his hand on her waist, burning as never before" (236). She rejects "John, peace, serenity, reason" (176), in favor of the hot-blooded Pedro.

When Rosaura finally dies, Tita and Pedro are at last free, "For the first time in their lives they were free to love each other openly" (241). In the final scene with Pedro, Tita, in a chile-induced epiphany, realizes she should not have wasted her life letting her emotions be controlled by reason just as "an amorous climax carried both toward the lost Eden" (244). Tita at last releases her long-repressed emotions, an event which sparks a purifying conflagration which destroys Tita, Pedro, and the ranch, a sacrificial atonement for the original sin of reason which returns the ranch to its pristine edenic purity, "converting that land into the most fertile of the region" (244). The lesson is clear: when a culture is forced by reason to sublimate its emotional life, sooner or later it must encounter an apocalyptic final moment, a cataclysmic and purging return of the repressed.

In this edenic narrative the demonized gringo scientist is rejected, and so by analogy the "masculine" values of Western technoscience and instrumental reason, and the purity of the prelapsarian garden is restored. The *malestar* in the rancho—cold, repressive rationality—becomes a metaphor for the *malestar en la cultura* in Latin America.[9] In the either/or world of the novel, the two value systems, gringo reason and indigenous emotion, are posited as mutually exclusive binary oppositions. The director of the film version of *Like Water for Chocolate*, Esquivel's husband Alfonso Arau, explains his cinematic vision of the relation between these two "opposing" discourses:

> In this movie, the male mentality is identified with the Mexican revolution and the mother, even though she's female. The heroine, Tita, and the maid Nacha represent intuition, passion, sentiment associated with the female mentality. And this film was about the superiority of intuition over reason. I am saying the brain is a very limited device. It's a very sophisticated computer, but intuition gets you in touch with the universe. (in Elias 1994)[10]

Arau's cybernetic metaphor notwithstanding, his description of the binary metaphysics of *Like Water for Chocolate* is fairly accurate. Woman's magic, representing intuition, indigenous knowledge, and emotion is opposed to gringo man's rational science and technology, with predictably apocalyptic results. The antidote to modern civilization is perceived as a return to an imaginary Edenic perfection before the fall into rational scientific knowledge, that is, as a return to origins and a more "authentic" mythical knowledge.

But how effective, in terms of the establishment of viable options to current relations between society and technologies of domination in Latin America, is the alternative worldview developed in *Like Water for Chocolate*? Certainly, many of the ideas in the novel—the value of local knowledge and appropriate technologies, the domination of one-dimensional technoscience—are valid critiques of Latin America's relations with science and technology. But the question remains—is a valid alternative offered?—and here some doubts need be expressed.

In the first place, the outlook proffered in the novel simply reverses the idealization of progress into its opposite, the idealization of a mythical past. This perspective assumes humanity can return to a "traditional" way of life and this time not commit the same errors that brought it to its present impasse, the ratio-technological world of capitalist exploitation. This vision of a return to nature fails to realize that technology is part of human nature. Luz del amanecer's investigations employ technology and represent the alchemical origins that eventually led to modern science. It is through technology that humanity realizes any project beyond mere existence, and there has never been a human society that has opted for mere existence. To reiterate a point made in the first chapter, as Ortega y Gasset (1945–47b) points out, humanity does not require simple existence or estar, but rather *bienestar*:

> life signifies for him not simple existence, but living well. . . . Living well and not simply existing is the fundamental necessity for man, the necessity of necessities. (328)

Another problem with the type of knowledge represented by the medical interventions of Nacha and Luz is the fact that it cannot be called into account by objective science. Thus it represents the same type of knowledge claims which occasioned the development of modern science. It represents an arbitrary and highly subjective authority that must be taken on faith, precisely the type of myth from which reason was supposed to emancipate humanity. Is the fact that the dialectic of enlightenment has produced a nonemancipating version of objectivity sufficient reason to abandon the concept of objectivity, or proof of the need to construct another type of objectivity?

In line with this, it should be observed that an edenic, antiscience metaphysics lends itself both to right-wing calls for a return to traditional values and a reactionary utopian criticism of technoscientific civilization, since with the rejection of the idea of progress these utopias can only be located in a nostalgic past, one of "traditional" values. As to what these traditional values represent, one may note with trepidation that the binary polarizations in *Like Water for Chocolate* involve the ominous categories of race, gender, and nationality.

Another difficulty with this view, given its propensity for nostalgic idealization of a mythical past, is that it cannot adequately deal with the question of humanity's historical horizon. Since technology is an integral part of the past, present, and future of humanity, any representation of that past, present, and future that cannot satisfactorily deal with technology is necessarily reductionist and so incapable of competently representing contemporary society and culture. Additionally, the construction of an idealized past is itself a product of our present technosocial context, a fact which makes said idealized past part and parcel of the ratio-scientific present it seeks to reject. This objection harkens back to the *crise de conscience* in anthropology described by Clifford and others, especially Derrida (1976) in his well-known critique (101–40) of Lévi-Strauss's (1992) "A Writing Lesson" (294–304).

Finally, the idealization of an unchanging past fails to come to grips with the central problem of Latin America's relation with technology, that of defining an appropriate relation with technologies of empowerment and liberation while simultaneously deconstructing existing relations with technologies of domination, all of this from within the context of a hot society, that is, in a society that is irretrievably thrown into the hot information relations of a society of mass communication. This problem derives from the fact that the only available models of long-term sustainable relations with technology are found in cool societies (Rappaport 1960; Sanday 1981). The examples of the integration of Being and beings taken from cool societies exhibit the paradigmatic forms to which the myths of a return to origins aspire. An essential difference between these and modern, hot, societies is in their respective forms of information retrieval and exchange, a difference based on technology. Hot societies do not require weeks or months of feasting, dancing, and so forth to "print out" their stored information. Therefore, information age societies don't protect themselves against new information as do traditional societies, but rather incorporate it at exponentially increasing rates. In the information age, social change is a structural component of the system. A societal model which does not account for continual change cannot offer a feasible alternative to the present sway of technologies of domination.

Therefore, in terms of providing a viable vision for the establishment of long-term sustainable relations between technologies of empowerment, society, and nature in Latin America, one must conclude that a model based on imaginary opposition to the stereotype of the gringo scientist exemplified in *Like Water for Chocolate* is not only counterproductive, but dangerously reactionary in its ominous racist, sexist, and nationalist overtones. Furthermore, as Antonio Marquet has demonstrated (1991, 59–62), the familial relations depicted in the novel are a version of the Oedipal narrative and kinship relations theorized by Freud and Lévi-Strauss, and so reproduce existing patterns of competition and dominance.

Whether or not one believes that literature should serve a social purpose, the simple fact is that novels such as *Like Water for Chocolate*, and their subsequent cinematic incarnations, do have an enormous impact on popular beliefs and attitudes, due in large part to technologies of mass diffusion. I would argue that it behooves us to pay particular attention to popular images of technology produced, marketed, and disseminated from within the technoproductivist apparatus lest the commodification of ineffectual critiques of technology comes to serve the dual purpose of perpetuating and reinforcing the current rein of technologies of domination.

This chapter began with Fortes and Lomnitz's assertion (1994) that in Latin America "science did not result from internal development; it is an imported cultural product." This assertion simply perpetuates the myth of idealized origins, of the way it never was. The truth of the matter is, from the Inca, Maya, and Aztec empires to Perón and Castro, domination in Latin America has always been achieved through science and technology. The challenge is not one of "creating a scientific community in an underdeveloped country," but rather one of creating a nondominating scientific community, of creating a technocounterculture. It is incumbent on writers, theorists, artists, activists, scholars, and critics alike to produce a viable vision of this type of community, one of democratic technologies of empowerment rather than colonizing, monopolistic technologies of domination. Constructing imaginary pasts that never were is part and parcel of the dominating discourse of science, as evidenced by the complicity, in the final analysis, between Esquivel and Fortes and Lomnitz in characterizing science and technology as foreign in "edenic" Latin America. Science and technology are not foreign to Latin America, but rather an integral part of both past and present domination, and of any future liberation and empowerment. Only through a technoliterate vision that accepts this reality can viable change be conceptualized and disseminated. The question that remains, then, is where are the visionaries to accomplish this, and why have we not heard from them?

4

Ecoscience and Ecotravelers in the Disposable World

In previous chapters, we outlined the role of scientific discourse in mediating Latin American narrative, from the scientific travelers and travelogues of the eighteenth and nineteenth centuries, to the human sciences of the twentieth century. In the final decades of the twentieth century the unveiling of the social roots of the supposedly "value-free" natural sciences, combined with a growing awareness of the negative ecological ramifications produced by some, especially commercial, scientific practices and applications, has given rise to a crisis in the discourse of the natural sciences. In response, the science of ecology has attempted to fuse key elements of the sciences of nature and the human sciences in an effort to salvage modernity's discursive grid. A new subject, the "ecotraveler," is now charged with revealing the "truth" of both nature and humanity.[1]

Costa Rican author Fernando Contreras Castro's novel *Unica mirando al mar* (1993) is located at the point where the old scientific discourses and their present eco-hybrid intersect with a new discourse, that of the communications sciences.[2] The context of this intersection is today's disposable consumer society. Within the novel, both the naturalist and the anthropological discourses are recalled in a scientific traveler/ethnographer who journeys not through nature, but through technoscientific consumer culture, which has become a veritable "second nature." The scientific discourse of ecology is present in the facts and figures provided in the novel's subtext of environmental impact studies, air pollution data, and so on, but actualized by the reader who inscribes these "objective facts" into his or her "green" narrative. The ecologically aware reader is interpellated as the "ecotraveler."

The novel questions the validity of these received images—the scientific travelers and the scientific discourses they represent—by emphasizing the role played by the context in which we perceive these narratives. Contreras Castro recontextualizes these discourses by reading them in a new Latin American context: that of a disposable consumer culture, with all its antihumanist and antiecological ramifications, mediated by an emergent scientific discourse, the cybernetic paradigm of the communications sciences. In this chapter I wish to examine the interplay of the various scientific discourses—natural, social, ecological, and communicational—which intersect in Contreras Castro's narrative.

In the second half of the twentieth century a new scientific revolution has occurred. This is what Anthony Wilden (1987b) has called the Shannon Revolution, referring to "the definition of information [as] coded variety" (303) by Claude Shannon and Warren Weaver in *The Mathematical Theory of Communication* (1964). In this cybernetic paradigm, the discourse of science has evolved into a new form that Ilya Prigogine and Isabelle Stengers (1984) have characterized as "the science of complexity" (131-290). This new informational/communicational/cybernetic discourse has produced a new type of social text, a new reality or hyperreality as Jean Baudrillard (1983) would have it:

> *It is reality itself today that is hyperrealist.* . . . Today it is quotidian reality in its entirety—political, social, historical and economic—that from now on incorporates the simulatiry dimension of hyperrealism. We live everywhere in an "esthetic" hallucination of reality. (147–48)

While Baudrillard's universalist claims are obviously extreme—hyperrealism is not omnipresent—there is no denying that information and communication sciences play an ever-expanding role in constituting our realities and, above all, our consumer culture. More and more, we can buy both the virtual and the real on-line. One can now journey to the virtual world of amazon.com to buy a real book about virtual reality.

The new communication/information paradigm marks an important turn in Latin American narrative, a turn away from the old "Archive" of scientific mediations that has long been the source of Latin American narrative. At the end of *Myth and Archive* (1990), González Echevarría, speculating on future developments in Latin American narrative, writes "if one form of discourse appears to be acquiring hegemonic power it is that of communication systems" (186). Referring to this new discourse he observes, in a final endnote, "there is a novel beyond those by the masters here discussed that would not be determined by the nostalgia of origins or by the longing for uniqueness and identity" (221n. 54). I would suggest that *Unica* is such a novel, a novel which reveals, ironically, that no one is *unica* [unique], that we are all indistinguishable receptors looking at the *mar* or sea of information—the "anarchive"—that surrounds and engulfs us.

In *Unica*, Contreras Castro turns the ethnographic gaze of science upon itself to show us the power and reach of the mediation of the new scientific metaphor—the cybernetic society—in the construction of the late twentieth century Latin American consumer society. By revealing the mediation of science in both Latin American narrative and social text, Contreras Castro indicates the degree to which we are all marginalized, all receptors of a one-way cultural flow. Although the novel at first appears to deal with "them" and not "us," we soon realize that the apparent differences are merely quantitative and subject to change at a moment's notice. The "longing for uniqueness and identity"—often conceived of in terms of the traditional Latin American binaries of city/country, civilization/barbarism, european/indigenous, and so on—is radically reposited in a disposable consumer culture in which the media "code" constitutes and homogenizes all identities through the very act of consumption. Identity itself is consumed in the consumer society.

Unica, which functions on a multitude of allegorical levels, deals with the supposedly "sub"culture of the *buzos*, those individuals who live by scavenging (*buceando*) the major garbage dump or landfill of the city of San José, Costa Rica. The dump, Río Azul, and the people who inhabit it serve as a microcosm of the social, environmental, and ecological problems, and costs, of our "disposable" society. In the finest ethnographic tradition, Río Azul becomes, synecdochically, an analogy of Costa Rican and international communication and exchange. From the political wranglings of those involved in trying to find a new landfill site, and those trying to make sure it is in someone else's backyard, to the wholesale dumping of insecticides and pesticides which are banned in the "developed" world, Contreras Castro highlights the interconnectedness of the social, economic, and political issues that contextualize the ecological problems represented by Río Azul.[3]

The inhabitants of the dump or *buzos* are, like everything else in Río Azul, the discarded products of consumer society. Since they no longer produce (for the market), society has tossed them on the trash heap. Nevertheless, as with most of the items relegated to the dump, the question of their usefulness is simply a question of context. In Río Azul these discarded humans form a microculture of their own which, ironically, throws away nothing and recycles that which appeared worn and outmoded, in contrast to "new and improved," in the world beyond Río Azul. The residents of Río Azul fill their basic needs with what they find on the dump. In addition to food, clothing, and shelter, the buzos encounter human warmth, solidarity, and love amidst the waste. The title character (not the protagonist, for that is Río Azul itself), Unica Oconitrillo, the archetypical Latin American woman, even finds a child, El Bacán, abandoned on the dump.[4] She "recycles" the child, raising him as her own. She also retrieves a husband, Momboñombo Moñagallo, from the landfill and recycles him as well. At this textual level, the inhabitants are seen to cling to "traditional" human and family values, "to sustain the appearance of a life based on bourgeois models in the middle of the biggest shithole in the country" (125). A facile reading of the text could misconstrue this as a nostalgic call for a return to the conventional family unit and traditional values. This is not the case, as these values are later shown, with the tragic death of El Bacán, to be unsustainable in Río Azul. Toward the end of the novel, Moñagallo, disillusioned by the child's death, realizes the values and social forms Unica and he have been clinging to are empty, a fiction: "family traditions, customs, motherhood. . . . everything, everything was false" (124). We see that eternal values and truths, like everything else on the dump, break down and dissolve in a kind of Nietzschesque "chemical reduction." In Río Azul, where everything is disposable, there are no eternal truths or values.

Moñagallo arrives at the dump by way of an attempted suicide or "identicide" as he calls it (9), a term which summarizes the rite of passage into *buzo* (read consumer) culture. Having lost his job as nightwatchman at the Biblioteca General (for denouncing the sale of library books to a toilet paper company), where he kept awake every night for twenty years reading the classics, homeless and unemployable he attempts to commit suicide by throwing himself into the back of a garbage truck. This inept symbol of humanistic erudition fails in his attempt and winds up on the trash heap, along with the rest of society's useless (non-productive) junk. Said emissary of the liberal arts tries to organize and politicize the "masses" of the dump, "spouting fantasies of progress" (44), with laughable (non)results. The other *buzos* correctly define his enlightenment vision of a better world through progress as the fantasy of an old fool: "bottom line, he was going senile" (98). Modernity's central tenets—Progress, Emancipation, Reason—are, in the person of Moñagallo, relegated to the dump.

In addition to being a parodic symbol of humanism, Moñagallo represents the voice of author-ity, that is, the voice of Contreras Castro as an-thropologist, as intermediary between society and the "Other" of the *buzo* culture of Río Azul. Much as Lévi-Strauss traveling abroad in *Tristes tropiques* or Freud visiting the unconscious, the author, as the character Moñagallo, travels to another place to discover something whose presence at home has become unrecognizable.[5] As Moñagallo, Contreras Castro goes to the *terra incognita* of science, the darker side of the scientific "other," to discover and make visible the hidden discourse of science. Through Moñagallo's experience in the heretofore unknown culture of the *buzos*, we are afforded a new perspective on our own technoscientific consumer culture. At the level of observations or fieldwork, the ethnographic model at first appears to be viable. But it will later break down as the novel ques-tions the epistemological ground of the "author"itative conclusions derived from these observations. That is, when the novel questions the discourse of scientific method and its claim to an objective ground outside its own so-cial context. When El Bacán dies Moñagallo and Unica relive anthropology's *crise de conscience* in the sudden realization that their received values are a myth or *fábula*. They leave Río Azul to journey to a small town on the coast, Puntarenas. There they discover that nothing has changed, that they are still "inside" the discourse represented by Río Azul.

Moñagallo embodies the field worker-theorist in the classic model of a Bronislaw Malinowski, a Margaret Meade, or a Marcel Griaule.[6] Validated by "legitimate" knowledge acquired at the Biblioteca General, he lives with the "natives" of Río Azul, learns their "language," records their ceremo-nies, gestures, and behavior and in so doing constructs, within the novel, an ethnography of the culture of Río Azul. Finally, he uses his ostensibly keen powers of observation and analysis to create a solution to their "problems."

Moñagallo's solution is to work through the system, by means of protest marches and an abortive letter-writing campaign, to provide the traditional humanist solutions: jobs, educational opportunity, social services, and land reform for the *buzos*. The irony is, of course, that he is trying to work through the same system that created and perpetuates the Río Azuls and *buzos* of this world. His ridiculous efforts meet with resounding failure. But until the end, he fails to grasp that a disposable society is by definition inimical to any form of net recycling. To achieve stability, the market must continually expand. The old must give way to the new to avoid stagnation, recession, crisis. The figure of Moñagallo becomes a parody of the classic ethnographer and of the modern social scientist. All of Moñagallo's inter-pretations are skewed due to the epistemological and ideological constraints of his "method." He sees himself as an objective observer of *buzo* society, but the truth is he is the subject of *buzo* society—he is a *buzo*.

The professional ethnographer serves to translate the discourse of the "other" into terms we can understand. The ethnological model seeks to demonstrate some great underlying knowledge that the "primitive" has but of which he is unaware. In *The Elementary Forms of Religious Life* Durkheim discovers the principle of contemporary ethics and social theory in the sacrificial practices of the Australian Arunta, while in *Totem and Taboo* Freud discovers the fundamental principles of psychoanalysis in an imaginary primitive horde. In *Unica*, Moñagallo, in a satiric parody of the ethnographic model, simply projects his own received ideas onto the *buzos*. In the process, he gets it all wrong. They don't understand him and he completely misunderstands them. Moñagallo illustrates the paradox of the humanist or social scientist. He is simultaneously subject and object of his own discourse of knowledge. The *buzos* are not the "exotic" other but a startling mirror image of Moñagallo. He still thinks the homeless *buzos* are somehow qualitatively different from him, and so maintains an imaginary self-image based on his "difference" from the *buzos*. In the novel he minutely describes the *buzos* or "others" without realizing he is describing himself. At rare intervals, as when he inadvertently glimpses himself in a mirror, reality momentarily breaks through his denial and he is confronted with his true appearance, that of a *buzo*, and with the frightening fact that in Río Azul (postmodern consumer society), the other in question is really "us": "at times it's tough to recognize myself in the little mirror Unica hung on the wall; I look at myself and I'm shocked" (26). Moñagallo's denial speaks to the imaginary difference constructed in consumer society between the soon to be discarded and the already discarded. As Moñagallo tries to disavow, but Río Azul proves, this difference is illusory when everything, and everyone, is ultimately disposable.

The true irony is that his personal perception is irrelevant. The *buzos* and Moñagallo are all trapped within the technoscientific discourse of the productivist economy. The failure of the ethnographic model is proof that it deserves its place on the dump. By placing the realist ethnographic model in the fictional context of his novel, Contreras Castro demonstrates the literary nature of this model. The reader sees that the supposed objectivity of ethnographical mediation, its method, was a literary conceit all along. Shorn of objective truths, ethnography becomes simply one more disposable narrative trapped within the mediation of the discourse produced by communication science in a consumer society.

It is his ironic, carnavalesque approach that allows Contreras Castro to paint a picture of the human tragedy of modern industrialized development without recourse to melodramatic, naturalist (nature knows best), neoromantic (the noble savages of the dump), or anticapitalist (capitalism is the root of all ecological woes) attacks. He does not seek to engage in a debate within the system, but rather to demonstrate the futility of such disputation (including the supposedly contestatory "practices of everyday life"). And, it should be mentioned, though he deals specifically with Costa Rican elements, the same situations he depicts in *Unica* are present among the *pepenadores* in Mexico City's *Bordo de Xochiaca* dump, the *favelados* working São Paulo's *Depósito Municipâo*, and, in fact, all across the "developing" world.[7] Also, in a more ominous note, we are reminded of the connection between *buzos* and "*desaparecidos*" which, though only implied in the novel, has been made explicit in landfill scenes in films such as John Dugan's *Romero* and Oliver Stone's *Salvador*.

The *buzos* realize that they are doomed to marginalization, but still cling to the empty forms and structures of society: Christmas, weddings, birthday gifts, and other symbols of their consumer religion. Unica, who has neither electricity nor television, goes so far as to adorn her hovel with that ultimate icon of the church of the media, a useless television antenna. The *buzos* faithfully reproduce the models elaborated by the media because they have no alternatives. They are passive receptors of a social text constructed by a faceless class of professional technocrats. There is no "outside," no empty page on which to write their own social text. Even their own bodies are already written by the toxic messages (a modern version of Kafka's harrow) which continuously bombard them at Río Azul. Within consumer culture, by definition, no alternative culture can exist. "Everything" is commodified.

In *Unica*, the models or forms the *buzos* cherish are emptied of content. They contain no message. In the world of Río Azul, neither religion, nor the Left, nor science promotes a different future, a better world beyond the sordid reality of the present. (Nor does the right perform its traditional duty of offering a better world in the past.) The only future offered in *Unica* is a dystopic one, and in this sense the novel is postmodern. Río Azul lies outside any linear, and thus potentially progressive, temporality. Life in Río Azul is not postapocalyptic, but rather frozen in the apocalyptic moment, surrounded by the eternal present of the engulfing sea of consumer refuse.

The religious values that float on the poison sea of Río Azul are shown to be empty and archaic, "the old values they sell us with new prices" (68).

The church is represented, and satirized, by El Oso Carmuco, a *buzo* "priest" with postmodern simulacratic tastes. He prefers copies of which there are no originals, specifically the religious equivalent of blowup Ken and Barbie dolls. In his hovel he keeps the lifesize figurines used in the yearly Passion Play in order to engage in year-round passion play. This causes ripples in Río Azul's mar of traditional values: "The women *buzos* were less than thrilled with the fact that Oso Carmuco stored the `saints' in his hovel, because at year's end they always arrived naked" (58). El Oso Carmuco's desire is the simulacratic desire of the consumer religion that has replaced the now empty traditional (bourgeois) values to which the *señoras buzos* vainly cling like drowning creatures clutching bits of debris as they are carried off on the floodtide of Río Azul. El Oso Carmuco does not even hear their voices as he is swept away on the tide of consumer ecstasy. The ancient idea of revealed "truth," first replaced by the scientific method of experiment and observation, has now become, in the technoscientific disposable society, pure simulation.

In Río Azul, not only God is dead, but also those forms that sought to appropriate religion's content: first leftist politics and then science. From Vatican II and the Latin American Bishops Conference (CELAM) to Cardinal Miguel Obando y Bravo, Archbishop Oscar Romero, and Gustavo Gutiérrez the Catholic Church has been powerless before techno-consumerism. Other Latin American religious turns—*Candomblé, Umbanda*, Pentecostalism—have been equally ineffective at turning back the tide of the techno-productivist culture. The complete failure and perversion of the Left has put the hopes of humanity for a better future squarely in the hands of science. But herein lies the most telling turn in *Unica*. The new religion of science and technology has only Río Azul to offer as its vision of the future. The discourse of science turns inward to criticize itself. While one voice in the novel represents the ethnographer or the social sciences, another, seen in the constant flow of facts, data, numbers and learned journal entries—"oil studies, seismic intensity studies, and environmental impact studies" (55)—represents "hard" science. And this impartial, objective discourse of facts and figures tells us that science itself is powerless to change society.

In *Unica*, the discourse of science is inverted, it now speaks of catastrophe and no longer of progress. The more perfectly science functions, the more it turns against emancipation and humanization. Science is the problem and not the solution. The "mar" that is Río Azul is beyond reclamation or restoration, the two most popular North American ecomyths. In Latin

America there will be no return to Eden. Technoscience is a creation of society that not only society cannot control, but that now controls society. In this sense the distinction between *buzos* and non-*buzos* breaks down. Here again, Reason has, as Max Weber predicted, turned from controlling nature to controlling humanity. The *buzos* are not the "Other," but both a reflection and an integral part of our consumer society. It is not just they who are marginalized, but all of us, before the anonymous workings of a disposable society that is as far from our control and understanding as it is from theirs. We are all disposable. Río Azul is a sea, not an island. The products, images, and people of the consumer society are disposable junk long before the tidal flow of consumerism carries them to the *vorágine* of Río Azul.

In a world in which the printed word, in the form of discarded newspapers, books, comics, and so on arrives, along with the rest of the semiotic garbage (all garbage is text and, in Río Azul, vice versa), at the rate of eight tons a day, the information overload reduces information to noise. Río Azul is a landfill for ideas, "a place to forget the useless" (69). The inhabitants of Río Azul are powerless to respond to the one-way information flow. Much as the Church once ordered women to read sacred scripture but forbade them to write, (Sor Juana Inés de la Cruz was forbidden pen and paper the last four years of her life for having contested sacred discourse), and today's consumers of television programs have no way to reply through the medium that constructs our "culture" (one cannot respond by writing on a television screen), the information superhighway that leads to Río Azul is a one-way street. No messages can get out. There is no way to reply to the production of the Other, to the church of the consumer media. In this sense the communicational marginalization of Río Azul becomes universal. We are all trapped in a sea of disseminated information, with no closure or anchorage save for the knowledge that we are constantly falling behind in the race to stay ahead of the curve. Like the *buzos* we are forced to make sense of a bewildering array of new information, whose only interpretive key is the admonition to keep moving, to keep scavenging. But we cannot predict the results of our uses of what we find. The majority of the *buzos* eventually succumb to the lethal effects of the toxic information they retrieve from the informational sea of Río Azul. Without access to a code or cipher, they must construct a reading of the text of Río Azul on the fly. And a misread communication can be fatal. There is no Robinson Crusoe to provide this army of Fridays with the tools even to read, much less respond to, the communications that arrive continuously. Río Azul is not an island, a clean sheet on which to write a new social text, but an always already written ocean. The marginalized cannot respond. Speaking of his adoptive son's plight, which represents our universal plight before the consumer media, Moñagallo says, in a letter to the president protesting the proposed closing of Río Azul: "What's El Bacán going to do? The only thing he knows how to do is read" (101). But the president never even receives the letter. The first person Moñagallo hands it to throws it away, because the idea of a *buzo* writing to the president, or to anyone for that matter, is inconceivable. Only the technocrats, the *clercs*, have the key of writing, the power to construct the social text.

The problem in Río Azul is that the feedback loops in the communicative circuit have been severed, if they ever existed in the first place. Moñagallo's protests and letters are not received as information but as noise. Both inside and outside Río Azul they have no meaning whatsoever. The informational-communicational model of modern science began with and is predicated upon the science of cybernetics. The new science of ecology, the supposed antidote to Río Azul, is also based upon the cybernetic concept of feedback loops (the theory of succession). But for the marginalized, the receptors of the one-way flow produced by the consumer media, there is no feedback. Ecological warnings are just one more bit of information coming down the one-way infobahn. In *Unica*, the cybernetic society is disconnected. It moves forward on its own. If there were once subjects to write the story of "progress," it now writes them. The system controls and uses the technocrats it creates to produce yet more social text. The cybernetic society feeds back upon itself in an exponentially expanding spiral of simulacra, divorced from the Real. Consumer culture is not in an essential relation of feedback with either the consumer or the environment. The *buzos* can only read (consume).

The social text produced by the technocrats once represented, in modernist discourse, the hope embodied in the combined powers of science and technology, a vision of "progress" seen in Latin America from the *cientifistas* of the Porfiriato to the bureaucratic-authoritarian regimes of Brazil and the Southern Cone.[8] But, unlike the "true" science heroically portrayed in another commentary on the role of science in Costa Rica— Steven Speilberg's *Jurassic Park*—in Río Azul there is no "true" science to save us and no "normal," mainstream family to right the wrongs produced by renegade techno-scientists in league with capitalist consumer-society. *Unica* deals not with science fiction, but with science as creator of fiction, as textual construction and textual constructor. Río Azul is a symbol of the sea of techno-consumerist information/infotainment which has already engulfed us, Rivera's *Vorágine* writ large. In Río Azul there are no jurassic sauros to consume us. We are already consumed. The message is that it is too late, one cannot hold back the sea that swallows everything. In *Unica*, la Llorona does not throw her child into the rushing waters of a river but simply sets him down by her side for a moment in order to retrieve an object from the dump. In that moment the child is engulfed by the *mar* that is Río Azul and disappears forever. La Llorona consoles herself with a plastic baby she finds on the dump, a simulacrum that replaces the real. The one-way information flow is not a passing river but an all engulfing sea.

A subplot in the novel, already alluded to, is a proposal to close Río Azul and open another landfill site. Río Azul is overflowing, and so a new site must be found. But there are no acceptable alternatives. It is a double bind. The market must simultaneously expand and not expand. In this situation we see the contradiction inherent in the scientific discourse that mediates consumer society: the need for infinite growth in a finite world. The scientific ship named "Infinite Progress" has run aground on the finite shoals of the mar called Río Azul.[9] The scientists at the university advise against a proposed location for the new garbage dump, while the company that is to build it provides a positive study: "Nothing to worry about, the place was so perfect for a garbage dump that it's hard to explain why one didn't evolve there naturally from the beginning of time" (112). There are protest marches and demonstrations, but in the end none of these oppositional voices matter. The debate is rendered moot by the interminable and inescapable rising tide of consumerism, "there were no alternatives, there was simply no place to dump the garbage, end of discussion" (113). The relentless flow of the river of techno-productivism, ironically called Río Azul, cannot be checked and so overrides all other considerations. Science can no longer control its own production. Every attempt to fix the old ecological calamities brings new catastrophes, which multiply at an ever expanding exponential rate, like compound interest or cancer cells. And all the while, science can offer no solution, for it is part of the problem. The discourse of ecology turns in on itself to become simply one more disposable commodity.[10] It has no use value, only exchange value. The discourse of ecology produces either publications, the medium of exchange in the economy of the university, or favorable environmental impact reports, which are converted into profit in the corporate economy. In either case, the discourse of ecology produces only disposable equivalents of exchange, commodities that ultimately come to rest in Río Azul. The very notion of science as objective or "context-free" is shown to be its undoing. This notion enables science to be disconnected from its social context, reified, and then commodified.

The only ray of hope occurs near the end of the novel when Unica, unable to speak (to reply) since the death of El Bacán, and Moñagallo leave the sea of garbage at Río Azul, the *mar* Unica has been looking at throughout the novel, and go to the other sea, the real one at Puntarenas. Here they eke out a humble existence *buceando* the local garbage, a move which seems to imply something of "small is beautiful" (E. F. Schumacher) or an "appropriate technologies" theory.[11] But their modest hope is swallowed effortlessly by the omnipresent sea of consumer production that surrounds them. Effectively, they are still "inside" Río Azul. They cannot escape Río Azul either figuratively (they are still trapped within the disposable society) or literally (toxins from Río Azul have contaminated the aquifer at Puntarenas). At the end of the novel Unica tosses the petals of a red rose, one by one, onto the sea at Puntarenas. The rose, the one thing of beauty in the novel, disappears without a trace into the immensity of the sea.

I believe *Unica* marks an important turn in Latin American narrative in several ways. First of all, it reminds us of the importance of the discourse of science in the construction of Latin American narrative, social, and cultural texts. *Unica* is a historiography of the mediation of scientific discourse in Latin American narrative and social text. There has long existed a prejudice in cultural studies to valorize popular (multi)culture. Implicit in this valorization is the rejection of "unpopular culture"—the purview of a supposedly nonmarginalized group—the "other" of C. P. Snow's two cultures or Francis Bacon's two tribes. In their zeal to reject modernity's hegemonic discourse the ethnographers of popular culture have repeated the strategy they seek to deconstruct and have marginalized the "other" of popular culture, namely science.[12] But, as *Unica* reminds us, science, through experiments and the applications of experimental results, constructs and verifies the images that constitute our culture, or "worldpicture" as Heidegger would say. This process culminates in the science and technology of information. It is the centrality of a new Latin American reality—the mediation of consumer culture by the communication sciences—that is foregrounded in *Unica*.

The novel recalls an earlier debate on the predicted affects of the "society of mass communication." One view, represented by Theodor Adorno in works such as *The Dialectic of Enlightenment* (with Max Horkheimer) and *Minima Moralia*, argued that the means of mass communication would, essentially through the widespread dissemination of propaganda, produce a homogeneous, Orwellian "Big Brother" society, a "narrative of monoculture." A contrary view, of which Jean-François Lyotard's position is representative (1984), argued that mass communication would produce a dissolution of centralized perspectives or "grand narratives," and a concomitant proliferation of *Weltanschauungen*. Antonio Benítez Rojo's position on "postmodern transculturation" in *La isla que se repite* [The Repeating Island] (1989), discussed in the next chapter, reflects a Latin American variant of this view. It is this second perspective which has enjoyed recent good fortune. An important feature of *Unica* is that it reformulates this debate in a new context. In *Unica* we see the illusory nature of apparent "differences" when these are considered in the light of the dominating mediation of the technoscientific consumer discourse. The *buzos* come from all sectors of Costa Rican society—Unica was a teacher before the budget cuts—but are indistinguishable once they are immersed in the consumer sea of Río Azul. Moñagallo suffers an identicide and Unica a "voiceicide," both emblematic of the Consumer as constructed by the discourse of the disposable society. The romantic notion of an "exotic" other located outside the dominant discourse becomes problematic. Consumer culture effaces apparent differences. The *buzos* are not a metaphor of popular culture but rather of mass culture, of the "identicide" of the Subject. They are not outside the productivist economy but instead are an essential part of it. We are all *buzos*. This is an important statement about an emerging Latin American cultural reality.

Technoscientific mediation plays a central role not only in nonpopular culture but also in popular culture, from the television antennas that killed the traveling circus in Carlos Diegues's *Bye Bye Brazil* (1980, itself a techno-travelogue) to the images of Chico Mendes on North American television (*In the Name of Progress*, 1991, The Annenberg/CPB Project). Miami, Florida, is now the "cultural capital" of Latin America because it houses the headquarters of the television networks Univisión and Telemundo. *Unica* suggests that the apparent differences which exist at the level of popular cultures are today subsumed by the higher level mediation of communications science. Specific differences in the surfaces people present to each other cease to signify anything of much value when everyone's repertoire of actions, values, and ideas is constrained by the discourse of consumer culture.

I believe all parties would agree that the logic of the information market requires continual expansion, and hence converts "everything" into an object of communication and exchange. The question is, has the extension of the model of scientific "objectivity" (the real) to the world of disposable merchandise and images (Baudrillard's hyperreal), a move made possible by the technological reach of the information media, produced a multiplicity of cultures—an emancipation from metaphysics—or simply a multiplicity of images which are all messages in the same technoscientific discourse? My own reading of *Unica* indicates the latter. But of course my own reading is just that. The importance of the novel lies in the fact that it reposits the debate in a new Latin American context which emphasizes the centrality of consumer information technologies. Moñagallo's ethnographic narrative is important not because it demonstrates the literariness of ethnographic discourse, but because it demonstrates the technoscientific mediation of the narrative of the human sciences. Emptied of objective values, the narrative of the human sciences becomes one more disposable object of communication and exchange. The ecological debates in the novel are an endless series of papers and conferences produced by academic Moñagallos who are, like the humanists, both subjects and objects of the "context-free" knowledge they commodify. Their narratives are objects of exchange circulating within the academic incarnation of Río Azul, a variant mediated by the cybernetic sciences of communication and information.

If, as Nietzsche said, "The world itself has turned into a fable," what is the role of science in the construction of our present Fable?[13] *Unica* suggests the discourse of science and technology is alive, if not well, as mediator of many Latin American texts, both social and narrative, both popular and non-popular. The "pilot" or cybernaut that controls our technoscientific consumer culture is the discourse of science. We are all part of a marginalized silent majority written by the mediation of this discourse. There does indeed exist a "narrative of monoculture" against which the oppositional "practices of everyday life" are ineffectual at best. And this narrative is mediated by science. Contreras Castro suggests we, in a twist on Molière's oft-quoted Monsieur Jourdin, may have always been speaking (and spoken by) the discourse of science without knowing it. He further suggests we ought pay some heed to the discourse of science, for the boundaries of Río Azul do not necessarily end at the outskirts of San José.

5

Postmodern Transculturation

In his *Cuban Counterpoint: Tobacco and Sugar* (1947), Fernando Ortiz introduces the term "transculturation." Bronislaw Malinowski (1991) explains that Ortiz does so in order to replace various terms then in use such as "cultural change," "acculturation," "diffusion," "migration or cultural osmosis," and other analogous terms that Ortiz considered inadequate (657). Ortiz himself affirms:

> I am of the opinion that the word *transculturation* better expresses the different phases of the process of transition from one culture to another because this does not consist merely in acquiring another culture, which is what the English word *acculturation* really implies, but the process also necessarily involves the loss or uprooting of a previous culture, which could be defined as a deculturation. In addition it carries the idea of the consequent creation of new cultural phenomena, which could be called neoculturation. (Ortiz 1947, 102–3)

Thus, for Ortiz, transculturation describes a process of mutual, plural, and reciprocal influences between various cultures, a space of constant movement and dynamic interaction between complex open-systems. Angel Rama (1981), in his variation on the theme, *Transculturación narrativa en América Latina*, explains "the culture that receives the impact is not merely passive but instead offers a creative reply" (33). Therefore, the culture which is the product of the interaction involving the two (or more) participant cultures represents an emergent quality, "a new reality, compound and complex; a reality that is not simply a mechanical conglomeration of characteristics, nor a mosaic, but rather a new phenomenon, original and independent" (Malinowski 1991, 658).

Understood in this manner, the concept of transculturation makes clear the impossibility of applying the "analytic procedure"—the classic "method" of modern science—to cultural phenomena because these phenomena do not satisfy the basic conditions necessary for the application of analytic procedure: "the absence of interactions between the 'parts' and that the behavior of the parts be describable in terms of lineal relations" (Von Bertalanffy 1987, 17–18). From the point of view of Ludwig von Bertalanffy's early general systems theory, the forerunner, along with Norbert Wiener's pioneering work in cybernetics and Claude Shannon's achievements in information theory, of such present day sciences of complexity as chaos theory and nonequilibrium thermodynamics, an additive approach is incapable of describing the relations in open systems. An important consequence of this constellation of scientific advances has been to demonstrate the limits of Newtonian, positivistic science—especially lineal, deterministic, cause and effect—when dealing with open-system relations.

Viewed through Ortiz's transculturational focus, then, with its postpositivist emphasis on complexity, the open-system relations of culture must be conceptualized as more than the lineal sum of the constituent parts and so must be treated in terms of emergent qualities. For this reason, Antonio Benítez Rojo who, in *La isla que se repite: El caribe y la perspectiva posmoderna* (1989), broadens the focus of transculturation to include the entire Caribbean, suggests that the *Counterpoint* be considered "an early postmodern text" (159). By this he means that a postmodern concept of transculturation allows one to explain cultural phenomena whose interpretation eludes the analytic procedure—the classical and logocentric logic— of Modernity. Beginning with an examination of the model which "transculturation" replaced, namely its counterpoint *mestizaje*, this chapter seeks a critical inquiry into the nature of Benítez Rojo's postmodern cultural counterpoint.

Underlying the term *mestizaje* is an atomistic logic of race or national origin. The *Diccionario Porrúa* (1985) defines a mestizo as a "a person born to parents of different races" and defines *mestizaje* as the "result of a crossing of races." This genetic definition offers an excellent point of departure in that it so reflects the sociocultural codes that produced it. That is, the emphasis on an additive, genetic definition of race reveals the positivist/modernist roots of the concept of *mestizaje*.

In *Latin Americans: Contemporary Peoples and Their Cultural Traditions* (Olien 1973, 94-95), Michael D. Olien provides us with the following tables:

TABLE 3.1

Español (Spaniard) male mates with an *India* (Amerind) woman and produces a *mestizo*

Mestizo male mates with an *Española* woman and produces a *castizo*

Castizo male mates with an *Española* woman and produces an *español*

Español male mates with a *Negra* woman and produces a *mulato*

Mulato male mates with an *Española* woman and produces a *morisco*

Morisco male mates with an *Española* woman and produces a *chino*

Chino male mates with an *India* woman and produces a *salta atrás*

Salta atrás male mates with a *Mulata* woman and produces a *lobo*

Lobo male mates with a *China* woman and produces a *jíbaro*

Jíbaro male mates with a *Mulata* woman and produces an *albarazado*

Albarazado male mates with a *Negra* woman and produces a *cambujo*

Cambujo male mates with an *India* woman and produces a *sambaigo*

Sambaigo male mates with a *Loba* woman and produces a *calpamulato*

Calpamulato male mates with a *Cambuja* woman and produces a *tente en el aire*

Tente en el aire male mates with a *Mulata* woman and produces a *no te entiendo*

No te entiendo male mates with an *India* woman and produces a *torna atrás*

TABLE 3.2

Español male mates with an *India woman and produces a mestizo*

Mestizo male mates with a *Mestiza* woman and produces a *mestizo*

Español male mates with a *Mestiza* woman and produces a *cuarterona de mestizo*

Español male mates with a *Cuarterona de mestizo* and produces a *quinterona de mestizo*

Español male mates with a *Quinterona de mestizo* and produces an *español* or *requinteron de mestizo*

Español male mates with a *Negra* woman and produces a *mulato*

Mulato male mates with a *Mulata* woman and produces a *mulato*

Español male mates with a *Mulata* woman and produces a *cuateron de mulato*

Español male mates with a *Cuateron de mulato* woman and produces a *quinterona de mulato*

Español male mates with a *Quinterona de mulato* woman and produces a *requinterona de mulato*

Español male mates with a *Requinterona de mulato* woman and produces a *gente blanca*

Español male mates with a *Gente blanca* woman and produces a *casi limpios de su origen*

Mestizo male mates with an *India* woman and produces a *cholo*

Mulato male mates with an *India* woman and produces a *chino*

Español male mates with a *China* woman and produces a *cuateron de chino*

Negro male mates with an *India* woman and produces a *sambo de indio*

Negro male mates with a *mulata* woman and produces a *zambo*

TABLE 3.3

A. Legal condition:	B. Social Status:
1. "Spaniards"	1. Peninsular Spaniards
2. Amerinds	2. Creoles (New World Spaniards)
3. Mestizos	3. Mestizos
4. Free Negroes, Mulattoes	4. Mulattoes, Free Negroes
5. Slaves	5. Slaves
	6. Amerinds

For our purposes, the interesting feature of these tables is their additive and unilinear nature. As we can see from them, the equation "Spaniard plus Indian" gives as its product a mestizo, as though a mestizo could be fully described if only one had a complete knowledge of the constituent parts, the social science equivalent of Laplace's demon. From an open-systems perspective, a mestizo, the same as a Spaniard or an Indian, is a complex web of relations, a complex, emergent open-system which is more than the sum of the parts, more than the mere "mechanical agglomeration" of two racial "halves." The conceptualization of the mestizo and of *mestizaje* found in these tables, one that dates back to the positivist roots of the term, does not take into account the ongoing, dynamic cultural interaction between (oversimplifying for the sake of example) "Indianness" and "Spanishness." The resultant reductionism serves to justify the marginalization of the mestizo as "less than"—see Table 3.3, column B, *Social Status*. This process of marginalization seeks to legitimize itself in a supposedly objective positivist/modernist scenario. In the words of Benítez Rojo (1989), the colonial mestizo project looks to "legitimize itself in principals of `truth,' `exactitude' and `justice' that we hesitate to consider absolute, but rather the product of crude manipulations" (151).

As discussed previously, with the demise of positivism following World War I, the discourse of the scientific observer whose objective "method" qualifies him to comprehend the New World and reveal its truth gives way to an anthropological discourse which seeks to find new ways to rebuild a shattered world. In cultural theory this move produces a reconciliatory revision in the conceptualization of *mestizaje*, the paradigmatic example of which is José Vasconcelos's *La raza cósmica*. Vasconcelos's interpretation can be summarized as the opposite pole, the complete refutation, of the positivist/Eurocentric vision of *mestizaje* seen in Olien's Tables (1973). Vasconcelos (1972) sees in *mestizaje* not something "less than" but rather the promise of a utopian future and the revindication of the mestizo's mixed racial heritage.[1] He seeks to transcend the racial binaries in a proposed utopia in which a "fifth race, or 'raza cósmica' composed of the final mixing of all the peoples of the world" (235) will rule. In Vasconcelos's utopia, a kind of racial and spiritual "El Dorado" located in the future:

> unity will be achieved by the triumph of loving fecundity, and thus the elimination of considerations of racial purity. In such a way, will be engendered a racial synthesis that joins the treasures of all heritages in order to give expression to one unified voice. (235)

Vasconcelos valorizes *mestizaje* and censures that which is not a racial mixture by inverting the dogmatic values of racism, the binary poles of "pure" and "mixed" blood. According to David Foster (1983), "*Raza*, in its most general terms, is the glorification of what was traditionally believed to be the major defect of Latin America—its racial mongrelization" (74). By emphasizing the "strategic rhetorical inversion of the prevailing dogmas" (76) on the part of Vasconcelos, Foster underscores the modernist roots of *Raza*. Foster goes on to note "the opposition in the discourse of Vasconcelos to all documental tendencies" (72) in favor of "anti-intellectual concepts" (72) and the inversion of the two poles of the supposed "binary opposition" reason/emotion by Vasconcelos:

> If the United States repudiates Latin America because it is more emotional and not sufficiently intellectual, for Vasconcelos, the best quality of Latin America is precisely the primacy of the spiritual over the cerebral. (75)

Vasconcelos's version of *mestizaje*, though at first glance appearing to reconcile "opposites," actually deals with Latin American culture from an analytic viewpoint, that is, from the point of view of a modernist, totalizing, and binary analytic logic. Although Vasconcelos attempts to reject the rational and flee to the irrational, in the process he finds himself obliged to employ a modernist strategy which consists essentially in negating the other pole of the supposed binary oppositions (which he uncritically accepts as givens) in order to achieve his rhetorical inversion. His procedure follows the analytic principal of noncontradiction: P v ~P. Indeed, as Foster (1983) points out, the strategy of supporting the "other" pole has a long tradition in hispanic letters: "Vasconcelos places himself in a tradition made famous in Spanish letters by Unamuno, one whose discourse defies point by point the criterion of scientific discourse" (68).[2]

In both formulations of the concept of *mestizaje*, the Eurocentric depicted in the tables and that of Vasconcelos, sociocultural analysis remains trapped within the context of Modernity. Neither the one nor the other can escape the necessity of basing itself on an organizing center or foundation, be it Eurocentric or mestizocentric.

Benítez Rojo's postmodern model of transculturation seeks to avoid a historical/cultural center. The notion of transculturation Benítez Rojo postulates purports not to approach the Caribbean from either a Eurocentric, Afrocentric, anglocentric, or mestizocentric focus. Benítez Rojo, a la Lyotard, asserts there does not exist one single center, but rather multiple centers of Caribbean discourses, a "multiplicity of 'local' rationalities." This formulation reflects the *crise de conscience* in structural anthropology and ethnology involving the revelation of their literary nature (Clifford 1988, 22), and the subsequent rise of poststructuralist theory. Concomitant with the fall from grace of the humanist discourse of the social sciences, a new cybernetic paradigm has emerged as the dominant discourse of science, a form that Ilya Prigogine and Isabelle Stengers (1984) have characterized as "the science of complexity" (131–290). It is this new paradigm, and especially chaos theory, that drives Benítez Rojo's formulation of a postmodern transculturation. The science of chaos deals with self-organization within disorder or chaos, that is, within the constant change in the relations between open systems and their environments, relations Benítez Rojo, in the case of the Caribbean, calls "the polyrhythmic chaos of differences and repetitions, of combinations and permutations" (1989, 64-65). Thus, for Benítez Rojo, the nonlinear science of Chaos provides the perfect metaphor through which to describe the complexity of Caribbean sociocultural interactions, one which is legitimized by science, while at the same time remaining faithful to an antifoundational epistemological tradition stretching from Nietzsche to Derrida and Lyotard.

In his gloss of Ortiz's *Cuban Counterpoint*, Benítez Rojo finds the central tenets of postsmodernism already in place. He points to Ortiz's effort to avoid "establishing a semiological hierarchy between two or more texts, given that no text has the capacity to capture the reality it tries to signify" (153). Also, Benítez Rojo emphasizes the lack of "author-ity" in the *Cuban Counterpoint*, pointing out that Ortiz seeks to "demystify the concept of 'author,' erasing the halo of 'creator' that modern criticism has placed on him" (153). Referring to the rhetorical strategy of the *Cuban Counterpoint*, Benítez Rojo writes "the text is conscious of itself and communicates to us the fact that what we might interpret as truths are, in fact, arbitrary decisions chosen in order to conform to the strategy of the discourse" (154). He then underlines Ortiz's strategy of "unmasking the mechanism that we know by the name 'binary opposition,' and which sustains to a greater or lesser degree the philosophical and ideological edifice of modernity" (155). He makes clear the importance of this unmasking when he adds that the binary opposition is "simply a discoursal strategy, given that the respective unity of the two poles that are placed in supposed conflict not only is quite apparent but is also subverted by the presence of 'multiple factors,' that is, by differences" (155).

Having clarified the demystifying strategy used by Ortiz, Benítez Rojo seeks to use this same "postmodern" strategy in extending the concept of transculturation from a Cuban focus to a Caribbean focus. His goal is to circumvent additive, lineal, and modern systematization and at the same time avoid seeking legitimization in either the analytic/scientific discourse of the West or in the more "authentic," mythical discourse of the Caribbean other since, within the constraints of a postmodern concept of Caribbean transculturation, a central legitimizing position cannot be granted to any of the multiple Caribbean and Western discourses.

At the beginning of *The Repeating Island* (1989), Benítez Rojo comments on two readings of the Caribbean, one by James Anthony Froude and the other by Père Labat. Contrasting the two readings, he points out that "Froude directs his attention toward the differences, Labat focuses on the similarities" (5). After indicating "the restrictive violence that all binary focuses impose [and] the ancient polemic unity/diversity" (5) to be seen in the relation between the two readings, he offers us another type of reading, "that of the Chaos type reader, but without trying to negate or repress the relative validity of the other readings" (6). Benítez Rojo asserts here that there always exist multiple valid readings, each with its own context. He argues not against a critical stance which would eliminate various readings, but rather in favor of a critical position that deals with both unity and diversity through a realization that change is a cultural constant.

Interestingly, having gone to great lengths to repudiate the binary fallacy, he chooses the celebrated case of Enriquillo in order to illustrate the importance of considering all sides of the equation in cultural matters. Enriquillo was born in La Española, a few years after the arrival of the Spanish. His father was the chief of a Taíno tribe, but Enriquillo was baptized and educated in the Franciscan convent of Santa María de la Vera Paz. Later on, he worked for a colonist, whose son, named Valenzuela, stole Enriquillo's horse and attempted to violate his wife. Enriquillo rose up in rebellion, and for thirteen years led a group of rebels operating out of the Sierra. Finally, the emperor Carlos had to intervene, offering Enriquillo a letter of pardon on the condition that he hunt down and capture the rest of the fugitives and rebels, a deal which Enriquillo accepted.

Benítez Rojo posits the question, Why did Enriquillo betray his fellow rebels? In his stronghold in the mountains he ran no risk from the Spanish, he had his wife and family, and so on. In other words, if he did not have to commit treason in order to save himself or his family, why did he do it? According to Benítez Rojo, it was due to Enriquillo's dyadic cultural identity:

> Enriquillo, culturally speaking, had an indian side and a Spanish side; he sought liberty for his humiliated and repressed indian side in the Bahoruco [the mountains], but there he discovered that his 'Indianness' was now irrecuperable. . . . his 'Indianness' gradually became an insupportable prison. Little by little, his 'Spanishness' began to remember the freshness of the patio of the convent of the good Franciscans . . . and eventually he began to consider his escape from the Bahoruca to the liberty of *over there*. (289)

Referring to the case of Enriquillo, Benítez Rojo sums up Caribbean diversity as a constant oscillation between a "here" and an "over there":

> "Caribbeaness" [la "caribeñidad"], even in its simplest and earliest form— the interplay of Taíno and Spanish cultures—is impossible, since it tends to seek out, be it with the body or with the mind, an "over there" that is alternately posited as a space of liberty and as a space of repression . . . there is an oscillation between utopia and paradise lost . . . therefore there are always groups that seek to recuperate African, or European, or Criollo cultural roots, while others speak of moving towards a racial, social, and cultural synthesis that is characterized as a "new" world . . . all the caribbean . . . finds itself

suspended . . . between the ground that goes from a "here" to a "there," and a clear sky that travels from "there" to "here." (290)

Evoking a sort of Lacanian split-subject, Benítez Rojo underlines his bicameral thesis by emphasizing the constant presence of the desire to occupy the space of the "other," the "over there," in Caribbean literature. One example, among the many he offers, deals with the relation between two books, *Historia geográfica, civil y natural de la isla de San Juan Bautista de Puerto Rico* (1778) by Fray Agustín Abbad y Lasierra, and *La noche oscura del Niño Avilés* (1984) by Edgardo Rodríguez Juliá. Concerning the novel of Rodríquez Juliá, Benítez Rojo notes the critics have observed that "the historical text has left its mark on the novel," that is, the novel is based on historical events taken from the documental *Historia* of Abbad y Lasierra. In addition, it turns out that the *Historia* contains a novelistic narrative that deals with a marginalized and nearly mythic figure, a certain Ogeron, the founder of Tortuga, "the city of violence and pleasure without limits" (303). Referring to the *Historia*, Benítez Rojo asks "How is it possible to explain the sudden abandonment of neoclassic prose and its abrupt replacement, with no transition, by a novelistic language very akin to romanticism a la Scott, but *avant la lettre?* Why this antidydactic treatment of Ogeron?" (301).

Benítez Rojo's answer is that Ogeron represents the "other" for Abbad y Lasierra, the repressed desire, the "over there" of the good Benedictine friar and Doctor of Theology. According to Benítez Rojo, Abbad y Lasierra "tried to legitimize the space of his prohibited desires . . . by giving a literary form to the adventures of the crazy libertine that occupied the 'over there' side, the 'other' for the Western Christian" (303). The documental historian wished to occupy the site of the discourse of fiction. Abbad y Lasierra wished to flee to the liberty of "over there."

The novel of Rodríquez Juliá is also a foundational text, but the foundation referred to is not that of the "official version" as in the case of the *Historia*, but rather the foundation of the "other," of Niño Avilés. The city founded by Niño Avilés, Nueva Venecia, is the cultural "over there" of the Christian West. It is the city of desire, like Ogeron's Tortuga. However, as we have seen before, it turns out that Nueva Venecia "has discovered that the 'over there' is no solution; it would like to escape from itself and flee towards the liberty of 'here'" (295). Niño Avilés realizes he is incomplete living a "mythical" life and desires a historical life. In order to explain the desire of the novel to penetrate the space of Abbad y Lasierra's *Historia*,

Benítez Rojo suggests that perhaps Niño Avilés "wished to write the measured and rational pages of Abbad y Lasierra, the pages that are studied and
esteemed as the origin of the 'here' of Puertorican historiography" (296).
For Benítez Rojo, then, in the caribbean the flight toward liberty is a kind
of "Strange Loop" (268),[3] in which the "here" is always searching for its
liberty in the other side, the "over there", while the "over there" looks towards the "here." This conflict is to be found within each individual:

> every caribbean . . . perceives his skin as a territory in constant conflict. . . .
> If one day the population of the caribbean were to reach the point where all
> were mestizo, the battle of the skin would not end; the conflict would simply
> be expressed in terms of matrices of color rather than in terms of black and
> white. (286)

For Benítez Rojo, the heterogeneity of caribbean culture does not imply
the coherent, continuous, and always self-identical "race of synthesis," "the
one unified voice" that Vasconcelos posits. Rather, the position of Benítez
Rojo is that *mestizaje*, or racial, ethnic, and cultural diversity, implies not a
fixed state of affairs, but a flow or oscillation, a constant movement toward
the liberty of an "over there" a constant motion between the multiple centers within the caribbean cultures and within the individual. In terms of
"the ancient polemic unity/diversity," Benítez Rojo appears to come down
on the side of diversity. In fact, given the apparent inescapability of the
here/there oscillation, unity appears to be an unattainable state of affairs. In
a variation on Freud's Oedipal sociology as articulated in *Civilization and
Its Discontents* (1984), each individual is characterized as a split-subject,
driven by the eternal return of the repressed desire of a "cultural unconscious." This essentialist position forces him to arrive at the same pessi-
mism regarding the future of the illusion of caribbean unity as did Freud, in
the larger sense of humanity in general, at end of *Civilization and Its Discontents*.

Returning to Vasconcelos's essay, under the light of Benítez Rojo's formulation we see that the utopia of Vasconcelos represents the "here" of his
Latin American identity. But according to Benítez Rojo, besides a "here,"
there must, minimally, also exist an "over there," and an oscillation between the two. The question arises then, is there an "over there" to be un-
masked in the unity of *La raza cósmica?*

Foster (1983), speaking of "the opposition in the discourse of Vasconcelos
to all documental tendencies" (72), concludes that "Vasconcelos implicitly
opposes the priority of science and systematic knowledge" (77) and that

"Vasconcelos plainly belongs to the tradition of antiscientific and antirational discourse" (68). Alberto Zum Felde (1954) also characterizes the essay of Vasconcelos as "fantasy" and "a fantasy novel" (426). But let us recall, following Benítez Rojo, the *Historia* of Abbad y Lasierra, the documental history that wished to occupy the space of the discourse of fiction, and whose author "sought to legitimize the space of his prohibited desires . . . giving literary substance to the adventures of the crazy libertine who inhabited the 'over there' side of his [Abbad's] Western/Christian otherness" (303). And let us recall also "Niño Avilés who wished to write the measured and rationalist pages of Abbad y Lasierra" (296) and the Nueva Venecia for which "its own 'over there' is not a way out; it would like to flee away from itself and toward the liberty of 'here'" (295). If Benítez Rojo's approximation is correct, there must be an "over there" within the *Raza cósmica*, an other that must, at some point, emerge. Where is the space of Vasconcelos' prohibited desire, the way out, the liberty of "over there" to which he must flee?

The answer—given his discourse so apparently antiscientific, antirationalist, and fantastic—is, obviously, science. Nothing could be more rational, more documental, or more modern than the unilinear trajectory toward the perfection of humanity that is science. And where is the science in Vasconcelos? In the very center of the imaginary amazonian utopia, given that the "conquest of the tropics," the realization of the "cosmic race," is based upon, and gives literary form to, the metadiscourse of progress, of science. From the very heart of the fantastic utopia of Vasconcelos surges the prohibited desire, the other, the "over there" of the cosmic, fantastic Vasconcelos. The road to El Dorado is paved with science, and in the heart of the fantastic darkness we find the enlightenment of Western science. Science makes the utopia possible, it is its foundation: "The fact that its coasts have few first class ports has very little importance, given the advances in engineering" (Vasconcelos 1972, 240). Science is capable of overcoming all difficulties. The utopia is located in the future because it must still wait for a few more advances in the trajectory of scientific progress: "The new race will begin to fulfill its destiny as soon as new means of combating heat are invented" (240). The new methods will come from Western science, "The science of the white race will someday utilize the same methods it employed to dominate fire in order to produce snow and ice" (241). It is clear that the "conquest of the tropics by means of scientific recourses" (242) implies not just technology, but also all of technology's concomitant projet, the *projet* of modernity, a truly Baconian *Instauration*.

Fleeing toward the space of mestizo liberty, Vasconcelos, by means of a Strange Loop, inadvertently also flees toward the space of repression, toward the same science that formulated the Tables of Mestizaje, toward modernity. Neither Vasconcelos, nor Foster, nor Zum Felde, all of them operating within modernity, see the hidden presence of the "over there" within the "here" of the cosmic race. For them, all relations must be P v ~P, either science or fantasy. But from Benítez Rojo's postmodern perspective, we are able to see both the science and the fantasy in *La raza cósmica* because we are supposedly "outside" the regulatory practices that institute stable, binary categories of identity and, most importantly, that impose the necessity to choose between the supposed binary oppositions.

But are we really outside the binary perspective? Looking out from the "here" of postmodern transculturation, can we glimpse an "over there" for which the desiring, postmodern, split-subject yearns? I think that clearly, given Benítez Rojo's exaltation of diversity, the answer is the "over there" of unity. Hidden behind the celebration of Caribbean diversity is the presupposition that diversity represents the "good," that somehow the various peoples of the Caribbean were once "whole" in their originary, prescientific, Edenic worlds. But at the same time, a leitmotif of *La isla que se repite* is the history of horrors perpetuated in the Caribbean by the clash of diverse cultures. Only a universal *mestizaje*, a unifying race of synthesis, can avoid the racial, ethnic, tribal, and cultural "battle of the skin." But from Benítez Rojo's essentialist theory of cultural instincts, the desired heaven of unity cannot be of this earth. If one accepts a postmodernist position which rejects any central, organizing discourse, then diversity and unity are necessarily mutually exclusive. In order to organize caribbean diversity into a coherent pattern, one need appeal to an overriding theory. And this is, of course, precisely what he does: invoke a general theory of diversity, in this instance chaos theory, a special case of the science of complexity, to explain the apparent disorder of caribbean diversity. So where Vasconcelos based his unity on Western science, Benítez Rojo uses the new metadiscourse of Western science to establish a unified field theory of diversity.

At the root of the double bind lies the presupposition that scientific discourse is somehow qualitatively different from other cultural discourses, and that the discourse of science is a uniquely Western discourse. By positing science as something on the outside of non-Western culture, as both Vasconcelos and Benítez Rojo do (while the tables invert the relation by situating non-Western culture outside of science), an essential binary is established that refuses unification so long as a methodological discourse

(Western science) is reified to ontological proportions (as objective reality). The unity that escapes the tables, Vasconcelos, Unamuno, Ortiz, and Benítez Rojo is that which would recognize the discourse of science as a contingent product of society, and not the other way around. The problem lies not in science itself, but rather in the institution of a certain *Ge-stell* or Social Imaginary that defines the relation of Western science and society in metaphysical terms.

For as much as Benítez Rojo's postmodern perspective may be accused of participating in the binaries here/there, Indianness/Spanishness, document/fiction, unity/diversity, culture/science, and so on that it seeks to escape, it must be praised for its contributions to the task of creating a new type of limited objectivity by elucidating a new scientific discourse, that of complexity. The scientific revolution of the second half of the twentieth century—von Bertalanffy, Wiener, Shannon, Heisenberg, Einstein, Planck, Schrödinger, and so forth—has opened the door to a new era of scientific discourse, and philosophers from Heidegger to Lyotard, and especially sociologists like Bruno Latour, have followed suit in pointing out the limits of scientific objectivity. Benítez Rojo's attempt to incorporate these currents into the stream of cultural criticism is important in that it points out (if inadvertently) the true obstacle to unity, the positing of science as Latin America's other and "outside," its "over there." Until a form of objectivity is accepted inside, there can be only oppositional diversity, and even "If one day the population of the caribbean were to reach the point where all were mestizo, the battle of the skin would not end; the conflict would simply be expressed in terms of matrices of color rather than in terms of black and white" (Benítez Rojo 1989, 286).

The problem is, and this is what has plagued attempts to theorize postcolonial studies from "outside" Western discourse, some form of objectivity is necessary. Without it, there are no subjects and hence no discourse, only the arbitrary revealed knowledge of a First Speaker accountable to no one, precisely the situation from which modern Enlightenment science, with remarkable success, sought to emancipate humanity. While much of twentieth century Latin American narrative, particularly magical realism, appears to argue for the archaic fallacy of an escapist return to *los pasos perdidos*, Benítez Rojo's perspective is situated in the contemporary discourse of the communication sciences. His postmodern perspective simply does not go far enough in its self-reflexivity to see that the discourse of science, the root of the oscillations of the cultural counterpoints—from revealed knowledge, to positivism, to the social sciences, and on to complexity—is simultaneously mythical and documental, and so represents the unity he seeks. The problem is not an objective discourse, but the objectivication of discourse, as Max Weber, Heidegger, and Adorno, among others, have pointed out.

An open-systems approach must remember that the theory of open systems is not itself a closed system. To describe relations between an irreducible plurality of cultural worlds by means of a scientific discourse located "outside" these relations is to forget that scientific discourse is itself a cultural enterprise. Cultural theory needs a form of objectivity which is neither completely objective nor completely subjective. Benítez Rojo's cybernetic, open-systems, communications model, which emphasizes the constantly changing multiple positionalities of a message-in-circuit perspective, seems to offer a promising way to accomplish this, so long as this model is located inside the cultural universe it seeks to describe.

6

Postmodern Visual Narrative

Brazilian director Walter Lima Junior's 1987 film *The Dolphin* [*Ele, o boto*] offers one variant of the widespread folktales, told from the rain forests of the Andean countries to the Caribbean basin, about the metamorphosis of dolphins into human beings. Although there are as many renderings of these stories as there are storytellers, most of these accounts share several common elements, among them the enchanted dolphin or *encantado*'s proclivity for attending regional *festas* dressed in stylish white suits in order to seduce local women and so father half-human children. Indeed, these are precisely the features Lima's interpretation takes as its point of departure.

The Dolphin is, at one level, the story of a love affair between protagonist Tereza Amaro (played by Brazilian soap-star Cássia Kiss) and an *encantado* or dolphin-man (portrayed by Carlos Alberto Riccelli). Tereza is seduced by the *encantado* and gives birth to a half-human/half-*boto* son, who is released into the sea the very night of his birth. Soon thereafter, Tereza's aunt María and cousin Luciano arrive unexpectedly to live with the family and share their humble lifestyle as poor fisherfolk on Brazil's poverty-stricken northeast coast.

After the death of her father Zé Amaro, Tereza agrees, due in part to financial exigency, to marry a member of the local gentry, a well-to-do businessman named Rufino Bare. Importantly, she marries him not for love but for protection, presumably from the *boto* and all he represents. At the festival of São João, the *encantado* reappears to seduce local young women, nearly enchanting Tereza and eventually claiming her younger sister Corina. Later, he appears at the wedding of Tereza and Rufino to destroy the wedding party by magically creating a hugely powerful, but mysteriously localized wind, "A passionate wind that only Tereza understood." In this instance, and throughout the film, the *boto* is clearly linked to the elemental forces of Nature and desire, man's irrational animal side of emotion and sexuality, and so the other of civilization against which helpless, and possibly complicit, women must be protected and regulated in order to maintain the civic order.

During the festival of São João, Tereza flees to Rufino's side for protection when she spots the Bacchanian *boto*, and the men of the village band together to cudgel a stranger thought to be, incorrectly it turns out, a *boto*. In another instance of the social order versus the *boto*/Nature, the men unite in an attempt to drive the *botos* from their fishing grounds, blaming them for chasing the fish from the area.[1] Finally, much as the Greeks assembled to rescue Helen from Paris, the men come together to hunt down the *boto* after he lures Tereza from the Bare home. This time it is at the insistence of Rufino, and the chorus of fishermen would have us believe that many are participating more for the free gasoline Rufino is providing than out of civic duty. This third instance of social cooperation, of uniting against the common enemy to protect Rufino's "property," is a more cynical one showing, as it does, the pragmatic self-interest that lies beneath the appearance of selfless communal sacrifice and collaboration.

Throughout the film, the phallic symbolism of the *boto* is aligned with Dionysian desire, passion, and libidinal instinct, while the village men represent Apollonian reason, civilization, and repressed desire. Indeed, the *boto* figure has much in common with that of Dionysus. It should be remembered that in Greek folktales and literature Dionysus represented the dissolution of established polarities. He is an Olympian god who appears in the bestial form of bull, snake, or lion. He is a male god, but he has a sensuality and an emotionality associated with women. He is a Greek, but he comes from barbaric Asia, and he is neither child nor man, but rather a sort of eternal adolescent. In short, he is the Other who represents all that is threatening to the stable order of the polis, all that confuses the basic antinomies which demarcate the human, rational, and civilized world from the alien, chaotic, uncontrollable, and bestial realm of nature, a predicament superbly illustrated in Euripides' *Bacchae*.

Dionysus also represents the other within that must be repressed, the unconscious desires, emotions, and instincts that must be controlled lest they tear apart the fragile fabric of civilization. For many, and epitomized by Nietzsche in *The Birth of Tragedy*, this Dionysian melody is the hidden locution of tragedy. Charles Segal (1978), in "Sex Roles and Reversals in Euripides' *Bacchae*," writes "The Dionysian myth of the *Bacchae* and the

Dionysian form of tragedy here work together to enable this 'anti-culture' to come forth from unconscious to conscious knowledge" (190). On this view, these tales are a manifestation of deeper human truths, the eternal return of repressed desires and fears which threaten to collapse the hierarchical structure of social difference.

In the course of the film, the *boto* surfaces yet again in order to make friends with Tereza's husband Rufino. This time the *boto* appears in the guise of a rich *gringo* investor whose plans to build a lavish tourist hotel on the Bare property promise to make Rufino a rich man. Rufino's cupidity leads him to invite the *boto* into his own home, where Tereza is very nearly seduced again. Indeed, shortly thereafter the *boto* entices Rufino from the home and subsequently eludes him in order to then lure Tereza to the beach and ultimately accomplish his task, leading to the *boto* hunt alluded to above. Finally, Tereza's cousin Luciano who, it turns out, is really her half-human/half-*boto* son returned kills the *boto*—his father—but in the process becomes a *boto* himself. These two sacrificial offerings, the patricide and Luciano's subsequent metamorphosis or sacrifice of his human half, propitiate Nature (and the culture that constructs Nature) and so enable Luciano to lead the other *botos* from the area, simultaneously protecting the women and allowing the fish to return, thus assuring the continued existence of the village and its way of life. In this manner, Luciano fills the messianic role of sacrificial victim or scapegoat that René Girard speaks of in *Violence and the Sacred*. Transgression of the social order must be repaid in blood, and the sacrificial victim is necessarily the "other," be it woman, foreigner, or beast, the *pharmakos* onto whom the violence that would normally erupt within society may be displaced (Girard 1977, 10-12).[2]

In addition to the Dionysian elements mentioned above, there are obviously Oedipal components in this family tale of love and patricide, and incestuous overtones do indeed pervade the relation between Tereza and her cousin/son Luciano, who in one scene professes his love for her and attempts to consummate it, although, unlike Jocasta, she manages to thwart the attempt. Here it should be noted that Oedipus too, like Dionysus and the *boto*, represents the dissolution of established polarities. Oedipus is both father and brother, husband and son, seer and blindman, poison and remedy. These three figures represent a mimetic doubling which is, of course, the essence of the Oedipal structure, the doubling from father to son of desire, especially the desire for what the other desires. As is well known, various versions of the triangle of desire and its repression—cf. Freud, Lévi-Strauss, Jacques Lacan, Jerry Ann Flieger (the "Gaze")—have been extrapolated or doubled from the familial level to the social, and this is clearly the case in Lima's film as well.

In addition to the relationship between Luciano and Tereza, a love affair also unfolds between Luciano and his aunt, Tereza's sister Corina (read mimetic double), who is eventually seduced not by Luciano but by a proxy *boto*, a transgression which precipitates her suicide but, like the sacrifice of Iphegenia in Aulis,[3] enables the *polis* to endure. Her suicide is atonement for the crime of transgressing the civic order, and also prompts Luciano to kill his father and so lose his own humanity, but in so doing to drive the bestial from the civic realm.

The use of the Oedipal family as a *leitmotif* in the film, along with two surreal dream scenes involving *botos*, points directly to Freud's scientific analysis of myth, dreams, parapraxes and so on, work in which these representations or signs can be said either to reveal or to create an object known as the unconscious, depending on whether one believes the object was there all along or that it was constituted by virtue of representation. Freud's analysis of Greek myth, especially his reading of the Oedipal tales in *The Interpretation of Dreams*, is the paradigmatic example of the privileged status accorded Western scientific discourse vis-à-vis popular discourses, of the view that scientific knowledge is a special case, immune to its own demythologizing discourse. In *The Dolphin*, Lima contests the privileged position of science by not granting it an exalted position amongst the multitude of discourses given voice in the film—Greek myth, Amazonian myth, cynical realism, surrealism, parody, documentary, and so forth. In so doing, he asserts that the idea that the history of Western science or Reason is the history of an exodus from myth or *Entmythologisierung* is a myth as well.[4] Thus Lima adds science, and its corollary of technological progress, to the list of myths operative in the Brazilian Social Imaginary.

The path is a long one that leads to Lima's view that even scientific rationality is simply one shared belief or myth among the many that organize Brazilian culture. The Oedipal *leitmotif* in the film and its origins in Freud's positivism recall a nineteenth-century Brazilian literature mediated by the positivist discourse of the natural sciences, a propensity exemplified by Euclides da Cunha's *Os Sertões* (1902). As we know, beginning in the 1920s the discourse of the natural sciences was replaced by the discourse of the social sciences in a search for new beginnings from which to rebuild a fragmented world, a search which centered, particularly in the *tristes tropiques* of Amazonia, on myth and language as the bearers of the "authentic" knowledge of the Other.

This early mediation of the social sciences in Latin American letters incorporated Freudian theory, avant-garde movements of the twenties, and early anthropology and ethnography, as these various discourses converged in the search for national identities and in the attempt to incorporate the rural population with its "popular" or "folk" culture into the modern state. In the case of Brazil, this intersection can be seen in, for example, the Week of Modern Art in São Paulo (1922), Mario de Andrade's *Macunaíma*, and the entire *Movimento Antropofágico*, of which Raul Bobb (whose *Cobra Norato* deals with the dolphin theme) was a part, and to which the entire *Cinema Novo* is much indebted.[5] Indeed, the changing treatment of myth and "the people" in the social sciences and in Brazilian literature can be seen in compressed form in the trajectory of *Cinema Novo* itself from the 60s to the 80s—from an initial documentary tendency through a stylistic evolution going from critical realism to the allegorical discourse of tropicalism, including the "cannibalist-tropicalist" phase (Johnson and Stam 1995, 32–50).[6] All of these genealogical factors are cited and reiterated in *The Dolphin* and so illuminate and authorize Lima's representational choices.

Finally, in line with the Freudian imagery and its evocations discussed so far, we might also add that from a present-day clinical standpoint the *boto* tales, and especially the reactions to them on the part of the "subjects," can be described as culture-bound syndromes. This approach treats the belief that one has seen dolphins turn into humans and back again, and that one has had sexual relations with same, as a culture-specific manifestation of a more general syndrome whose origin is the unconscious (Simons and Hughes 10–15). In the psychoanalytic literature the relativism of the culture-bound approach is not questioned at the manifest level. Ronald Simons and Charles Hughes (1985) point out in *The Culture-Bound Syndromes* that if another culture "were to develop a cross-cultural scheme for the classification of undesirable=deviant='sick' behavior, it would include Type A behavior as a prime example" (11).

This relativism does not extend, however, to the concept of an underlying collective unconscious that produces the transcendental phenomenon known as myth. The problem with this type of relativism is that although it talks about separate mythological systems, it does not consider to which of these mythological systems the theory of cultural relativism or the concepts of myth and the unconscious belong. Much as in the Middle Ages when one could argue the number of angels that might fit on the head of a pin but not the existence of angels, today one can argue the quantity of

meanings that may perhaps fit on the head of a myth, but not myth's existence as a meaning-bearing sign whose origins are in the unconscious.[7]

Once one accepts that myths are culture-bound messages from the interior, it is but a short slide down a slippery slope to asking what the tales told
at the manifest level reveal about the latent levels of the collective unconscious of the societies and cultures that produce them.[8] The definitive study
of the dolphin tales, Candace Slater's *Dance of the Dolphin* (1994), takes
this psychoanthropological approach:

> Like a growing number of literary scholars, anthropologists, and historians,
> I have been especially interested in the larger question of cultural-confronta-
> tion and the subversive possibilities of apparently innocuous symbolic forms
> (9) . . . the Dolphin stories provide a privileged understanding of the mean-
> ings and mystifications upon which worlds are built. (6)

For Slater, then, these tales reflect neither "timeless" myths nor something akin to Schelling's self-referential "tauto-gorical" presences, but rather
a sociocultural response to the economic, social, political, and environmental changes and conflicts taking place in present day Amazonia. This
approach, following a muted Gramscian model, presupposes the counterhegemonic nature of popular discourse—"cultural-confrontation and the
subversive possibilities of apparently innocuous symbolic forms" (Slater
1994, 9)—as distinct from the Frankfort School model which saw the popular sector as basically a passive receiver of cultural messages.

We may usefully contrast Slater's more Gramscian and so Latin American approach with functionalist Eurocentric research of only a decade ago
which insisted on the top-down nature of mythic discourse, as in Froma
Zeitlin's (1978) "The Dynamics of Misogyny: Myth and Mythmaking in
the *Oresteia*," Gerta Lerner's (1986) *The Creation of Patriarchy*, and Sue-
Ellen Case's (1985) "Classic Drag: The Greek Creation of Female Parts."
On this latter view, myth functions to impose and perpetuate dominant sociocultural relationships. In other words, myth is the cause and society the
effect, while Slater has it the other way round. The psychoanthropological
approach, then, aspires to synthesize the symbolist approach of Freudian
essentialism with a functionalist approach *a la* Malinowski.[9]

Although Slater's view in some ways de-archetypalizes myth—it is no
longer both the cause and effect of "Patriarchy"—it still trades upon the
underlying psychoanalytic postulate that assumes myth to be a transcendental feature of humanity originating in the collective unconscious. This
view also assumes that the manifest level or literal folktale is a censored or

coded message that needs only to be decoded, by a "qualified" agent, in order to reveal a latent and "deeper" truth, Slater's "privileged understanding." By positing the universal existence of unconscious desires and their symptomatic narrative expression (e.g. myths, dreams, fantasies, and folktales), this theory tautologically accounts not only for the universal existence of myths, but also for their cause—the unconscious—and their effect, namely to express the content of the collective unconscious. Their various incarnations or contents are explained as the consequence of local contexts, and so we have a tripartite model comprised of the literal tale at the manifest level, and two latent levels, one diachronic at the level of local culture, and one synchronic at the level of a global or universal unconscious. Thus theory (or ideology), which is supposed to explain observed reality, becomes the foundation on which reality is constructed, the pre-existing model to which everything must conform. Rather than discovering an already existing object, theory creates it. Slater sees *boto* tales as context-bound responses to change in Amazonia, but sees her own reading of them as universal and transcendent.[10]

Following this "folktale as coded message in the present" paradigm, a local reading that necessarily suggests itself is that of the *boto* as gringo or foreigner who wreaks havoc in traditional lifestyles with the changes imposed by his money and technologically backed "progress." In fact, in *Dance of the Dolphin* Slater devotes an entire chapter to "The Dolphin as White Man" in which she develops precisely this conclusion.[11] In the film, just prior to his meeting to tempt Tereza's husband Rufino with the forbidden fruit of the tree of technological knowledge, the multinational *boto* is shown descending from a new hightech bus, wearing gringo regalia, speaking first English and then Portuguese with a gringo accent, and making his first pause to refresh beneath a Coca Cola sign (a company ironically listed on the credits as a sponsor, presumably in the name of culture). Lima's representation here does coincide with Slater's dolphin as White Man equation.

The method used by Lima to portray the *boto* is, however, far from the ethnographic field study method that Slater uses. Indeed, as mentioned above, an important feature of *The Dolphin* is the use of a combination of cinematic techniques—documentary, surrealist, and realist—to relate the events in the motion picture. The *boto* as gringo motif is merely one representation among many. For Lima, a reading of the dolphin tales as a reaction to technological progress or technoimperialism is merely one piece of the puzzle. By situating the discourse of technology within a multiplicity of other mythic perspectives and viewing it through the eyes of various subjects, he demonstrates that this reading is simply one more story, one more social construct among many.

Lima's multilayered representational method proceeds, at least in part, from an awareness of the problem of agency, the acknowledgment of the ideological role of the agent or subject of scientific discourse.[12] In Latin America, beginning around 1950, the official anthropological stories were undermined by the general movement for liberation in the postcolonial world, especially the Cuban Revolution, and the accompanying realization that the official stories tended to be ideologically complicit with First World hegemony in Latin America. Clifford (1988) writes, "Henceforth, neither the experience nor the interpretive activity of the scientific researcher can be considered innocent" (41). From this point on, anthropologists themselves become aware of the literary, rhetorical, and ideological nature of their representative practice, and indeed today anthropologists such as Michael Taussig and Clifford Geertz, in a self-reflexive metadiscourse, proclaim the literariness of their work.[13] This longing to disavow the authorative voice, the same longing we saw in Fernando Ortiz and Benítez Rojo, manifests itself in the multiple discourses represented in *The Dolphin*, indicating Lima's desire to participate in this new self-reflexive metadiscourse.

The move to self-reflexivity is part of a more general critique, beginning with Nietzsche, of the ideological character of modernist representation and its unilinear conception of history, its cult of progress, and so on.[14] Given the putative end of Modernity and consequently the foundational crisis mentioned above, how does one legitimize the relation between an object of study and the statements made about that object? Specifically, how does one validate a statement regarding the connection between dolphin and other myths, and a corresponding Brazilian sociocultural reality?

As we have seen, Lima's approach is to offer a variety of perspectives on the same events, a cinematic doubling of point of view, of myth, and of the *boto* himself, who appears in a multiplicity of incarnations. In the film, there is a presumably "objective" off-camera narrator who, together with a documentary camera style, gives us one version of the story. This narrator often interviews a group of cynical local fishermen, a kind of Greek chorus, who offer a pragmatic interpretation of events—for example, the *boto* stories are just a cover for otherwise unexplained pregnancies, an excuse for poor fishing performance, a way to dupe gullible believers, and so on. There are also two dream sequences, which presumably shed light on the inner motivation of the dreamers, Tereza and Corina, and recall the Freudian influence pervading the decoding of myth and folklore. And finally, there is the overall record of events recorded by the camera—the complete film—a succession of events that includes the dreams, the documentary interviews with the chorus, keystone cops chase scenes involving the locals and the *boto*, and all the other actions that take place in the film.

The overall picture the film paints is one of multiple perspectives on the "meaning" of the *boto* tales, a kind of historiography of the various approaches to myth, narrative, and film in Brazil. A postmodern reading would have it that this contradictory, even chaotic view makes it difficult to conceive of a *single* correct interpretation. If there is no objective reality lying beneath, or beyond, the images Lima projects, so much the better, for the disorienting effect of a multiplicity of possible readings of the *boto* tales is precisely what provides the emancipatory element in the film. From a postmodern perspective, by showing that the manifest/latent binary is susceptible to infinite regress, and that at each level representation is not value free but rather the contrary, meaning is liberated from critical authority, be it anthropological, ethnographic, psychoanalytic, or literary.

This implies, however, that the ideal of a common social self-consciousness—Benítez Rojo's "unity"—is unrealizable. In a world of multiple language games there can be only limited, or at least not univocal, understanding of social communication and exchange. Indeed, without a sort of neo-Kantian consensus in matters of signification, a hybrid society cannot find commonly constructed social ground. The solution, the unifying social thread seems to be, for Lima, the shared foundation of mythos or narrative, which is precisely the mythic and tragic message of *The Dolphin*. Both in form and in content, *The Dolphin* iterates the essence of tragedy: it is not the differences but the loss of them that gives rise to violence and chaos in society.

This is the notion of tragedy argued at length by René Girard in *Violence and the Sacred* (1977), and subsequently taken up by a host of scholars (cf. Segal 1978; Bushnell 1988). I emphasize it here to underscore that what *The Dolphin* does is communicate the essence of Western tragedy through time. By positing a crisis of distinctions Lima reiterates the tragic message, and by positing the Other, the foreigner, the one who is part insider and part outsider, part human and part beast, as sacrificial victim whose death restores the civic order, he replays the *kathartic* moment in which "mysterious benefits accrue to the community upon death of a human *katharma* or *pharmakos*" (Girard 1977, 287) since "The purpose of the sacrifice is to restore harmony to the community, to reinforce the social fabric" (8). What *The Dolphin* does is perpetuate the discourse of tragedy, in both content and form, through a postmodern multiplicity of perspectives which by its very nature reiterates the tragic crisis of distinctions. The postmodern crisis, Lyotard's dissolution of Grand Narratives or Clifford's *crise de conscience*, is in Girard's terms a sacrificial crisis:

> The sacrificial crisis can be defined, therefore, as a crisis of distinctions—that is, a crisis affecting the social order. This cultural order is nothing more than a regulated system of distinctions in which the differences among individuals are used to establish their "identity" and their mutual relationships. (Girard 1977, 49)

Once myth is accepted as a meaning bearing sign, and this meaning is decoded and a "truth" revealed then, given the incompatible variations of myth, it follows that by the principle of non-contradiction not all myths can be true. But this conclusion denies the postulate that all myth is a bearer of deeper truths. The obvious solution is to posit a theory of cultural relativism in order to recuperate the notion that all myths are equally true. The problem with this approach is, of course, that any contact with another cultural world undoes the separation that relativism needs. The effort to relativize—the postmodern move *extraordinaire*—provokes the embodiment of tragedy, a crisis of distinctions. Relativism becomes simultaneously "poison" and "remedy." Lima's solution is, as we have seen, to retreat to a restoration of differences, the *boto* is killed, the *polis* is delivered from the plague that caused the fish to vanish, and the hierarchies return.

Ultimately then, what initially appears to be a postmodern perspective in *The Dolphin*, the multiplicity of differences given voice in the film, becomes the paradigmatic tragic moment as narrative movement converts multiple differences into a crisis of difference in the measure in which these various differences interact and are put into relation with one another in the course of the film. Lima's solution to the crisis of difference is thus similar to that we've seen in many texts. The *boto*/other is sacrificed to restore the civic order, much as the rational discourse of science and technology, often portrayed as *gringo pharmakos*, is sacrificed in other texts to restore a prelapsarian innocence, an imagined authentic unity. But this unity is actually based on the preservation of a fundamental hierarchy of differences which is preserved through the sacrifice of that which threatens to annul this hierarchy. What *The Dolphin* does is perpetuate the foundational discourse of Modernity, namely the agonistic discourse of competitive differences, a discourse mediated in the specular realm of the Social Imaginary. So if Latin American society is to develop a new relation with science and technology it will not be through an agonistic narrative which sees technology as the *katharma* whose death restores the established hierarchy of differences.

The question of what narrative does, rather than simply what it says, becomes central as we move into new, electronically mediated forms of narrative. In the coming chapters, we will examine the possibility that technologically mediated, nonlinear, hypernarrative might produce a new social coding with the power to turn away from the *mythos* of Modernity and toward a recodification of the relations between society and its many environments. We will consider the possibility that the arrival of a new form of narrative might provide a viable alternative to the primordial, foundational narrative, that it might provide what Heidegger called a "Turning" or "a surmounting of enframing."

7
The Arrival of the Posthuman

In what follows, I wish to consider the possibility of arriving at a new social coding by means of the "new media." There are really two, interrelated concerns here: the possibility of transcending current embodied relations offered by the novel concept of virtual identities, a kind of "cybermestizaje"; and the potential social recodification offered by a new form of narrative, a nonlinear narrative created through the use of hypermedia. The central question to be considered is that of agency—human and/or technological—and the question of who or what has the power to change social coding. Is the arrival of the new media something so qualitatively different as to imbue the technological itself with agency, and so the power to effect social change, or is the posthuman future an illusion with respect to a possible end of Modernity's metacode?

In terms of digital media, a central concern is that of virtual identity. What happens to the identity politics of material bodies when we go online? We can begin to answer this question by looking at some examples of what happens when the ideal virtual world interacts, some would say clashes, with its real, material environment. A case in point is that of cybercritic Mark Dery, who ends his 1993 essay "Flame Wars" with an appeal to what Diana Fuss (1989) has called the essentialism of experience. The last paragraph of his article is a quote from a private e-mail message sent him by computer programmer William Rolf Knutson:

> I really have no objection to someone who has come into our community, lived here and participated, analyzing [his] experience and trying to put it into perspective. I think the objection to the "critics" who are now fawning over cyberthis and cyberthat is that they are perceived as intellectual carpetbaggers who don't bother to learn the terrain before they create the map. (Dery 1993, 567)

Immediately afterwards, we read under Notes: "I am greatly indebted to Gareth Branwyn . . . [for] his willingness to fact-check the finished work, sparing me the fate of the 'intellectual carpetbagger'" (567).

The recurrent effort on the part of Dery to establish his own authenticity is particularly interesting inasmuch as his article, while purporting to treat the vitriolic e-mail exchanges known as flame wars, in fact deals with the supposedly liberating anonymity of electronic communication and exchange:

> their authors are sometimes anonymous, often pseudonymous, and almost always strangers. Which is the upside of incorporeal interaction: a technologically enabled, postmulticultural vision of identity disengaged from gender, ethnicity, and other problematic constructions. On line, users float free of biological and sociocultural determinants. . . . People are judged on the content of what they say. (Dery 1993, 561)

But if people are truly "judged on the content of what they say," why the apparent urgency to construct an identity immune to the *ad hominem* charge of "intellectual carpetbagger," why the appeal to the authority of Gareth Branwyn (editor of the fringe culture 'zine *bOING bOING*)? Perhaps the essentialism of authority is not one of the "other problematic constructions" from which the "postmulticultural vision of identity" may be disengaged. And if the clear and distinct intellectual subject were left to "float free," what of the corporeal, the biological determinates Dery refers to? Does the material body become arbitrary and irrelevant for the virtual subject? Will eliminating the material eliminate the discourse of difference, or create a crisis of difference?

In "Will the Real Body Please Stand Up?: Boundary Stories about Virtual Cultures," Allucquére Rosanne "Sandy" Stone (1991a) offers two tales from cyberspace that illustrate the perceived perils of anonymity. The first story is about a totally disabled older woman named Julie, a feminine cybersubject who participated in women's conferences on the "net" in the mid-eighties, developing deep relationships with the other women on-line and offering "advice that changed their lives." However, as Stone explains, "After several years, something happened that shook the conference to the core. 'Julie' did not exist. 'She' was, it turned out, a middle-aged male psychiatrist. . . . It worked for years, until one of Julie's devoted admirers, bent on finally meeting her in person, tracked her down" (83). The women on the net felt "raped" and "violated" by this act of computer-mediated crossdressing, having assumed that "many of the old assumptions about the nature of identity had quietly vanished under the new electronic dispensation" (83). Although Julie was no intellectual carpetbagger, she was a corporeal carpetbagger.

Another of Stone's accounts deals with one of the first electronic bulletin boards, the San Francisco based CommuniTree #1, which went on-line in May 1978. The visionary CommuniTree system ensured both privacy (anonymity) and unlimited access to all participants. But by 1982 Apple Computer began to give away computers to public schools in the Bay area, a move which produced a bumper crop of young hackers, some of whom proceeded to avail themselves of the anonymity and free access of the system in order to repeatedly "crash" the network. As Stone reports, "Within a few months, the Tree had expired, choked to death with what one participant called 'the consequences of freedom of expression'" (Stone 1991a, 91). For Stone, the moral of the story is that "surveillance and control proved necessary adjuncts to maintaining order in the virtual community" (91). But what is the object of this surveillance and control? Is it the free floating point of view of the virtual subject, the young hackers, or the material body, as in the case of "Julie," from which this point of view emanates?

In "Performing Lesbian in the Space of Technology: Part II," Sue-Ellen Case (1995) seeks to synthesize the screening process and the computer screen, that is, to treat the problem of "passing" in the virtual community. Speaking of Sappho, an electronic bulletin board focused on lesbian issues and identities, Case considers the problem of screening the lesbian:

> "Performing lesbian," in this instance, signifies the composition of Sappho's virtual body/community, in its dialogic, electronic space. The virtual nature of this body, however, has inspired anxieties about the eligibility of its membership. Constituted as lesbian, but identified only by electronic address, how can the members be certain that no man is online with them? No heterosexuals? (341)

In this case, the problem is a combination of the possibility of unlimited access and the question of the material body. Both issues raise the question of surveillance and control. How to discriminate—between, against, in favor of—certain constellations of behavior without the visual cues that complete the pre-established semiotic codes for those patterns of behavior, that is, without the appropriate citations or appeals to authority—material or intellectual—that legitimize a given performance. How does one discipline and punish the oxymoronic "virtual body," how can citation be distinguished from parody without material data, without a body in/of evidence?

In "The Empire Strikes Back: a Posttranssexual Manifesto," Sandy Stone (1991b) reports the same resistance to her/his rewriting of the body that we saw in the examples taken from the virtual community. Indeed, the title of Stone's article is a response to Janice Raymond's 1979 book *The Transsexual Empire: The Making of The She-Male*, in which Raymond defends "true" (read: material) women against male usurpation:

> Masculine behavior is intrusive. It is significant that transsexually constructed lesbian-feminists have inserted themselves into the positions of importance and/or performance in the feminist community. Sandy Stone . . . illustrates this well. . . . The . . . visibility he achieved . . . only served to enhance his previously dominant role and to divide women. . . . As one woman wrote: "I feel raped when Olivia passes off Sandy . . . as a real woman. After all his male privilege, is he going to cash in on the lesbian feminist culture too?" (in Stone 1991b, 283–84)

Ironically, then, the virtual community of Sappho seeks to ground legitimacy in the material body—"how can the members be certain that no man is online with them?"—while the materially (surgically) transsexual Stone seeks a textual transsexual subject "grounded in the *intertextual* possibilities of the transsexual body. . . .we must begin to rearticulate the foundational language" (297).

As we have seen in previous chapters, in Latin America the question of "passing" and "screening"—of racial purity and *mestizaje*—has a long and tortured history. From the positivist/geneticist taxonomies that produced mindnumbing lists of possible combinations—*no te entiendos, tente en el aires, mulatos, cambujos, zambos,* and so forth—to José Vasconcelos' *raza cósmica,* Fernando Ortiz's transculturation and Antonio Benítez Rojo's postmodern transculturation, the construction of subjects has always been mediated by the material body. At stake have been the same legitimization and access to privilege that are contested in the present cyberculture identity wars.

Technoscientific advances have given rise to a new formulation for describing the present technoscientific moment, namely the concept of "hybridity." On the one hand, Latin American writers such as Néstor García Canclini use it to describe the splitting of the Latin American subject upon entry into the technoscientific world picture, while on the other hand First-World writers such as Katherine Hayles use the same term to describe the subject passing through the other side of the cultural divide to the "posthuman":

For some time now there has been a rumor going around that the age of the human has given way to the age of the posthuman. . . .Humans are not the end of the line. Beyond them looms the cyborg, a hybrid species created by crossing biological organism with cybernetic mechanism. (Hayles 1995, 321)

Some recent work of the Mexican writer Carmen Bullosa indicates the beginnings of a Latin American hybrid fusion of the posthuman and the *mestiza* into a sort of cybermestiza. According to Bullosa, the novel she is currently working on "begins with a third voice and it's a voice of a woman of the future. . . .They are post-humans . . . .she has no father, no mother, they have artificial parents, they are another kind of human" (in Reid 1995, 151). In her previous novel *Duerme* (1994), Bullosa highlights the theme of hybridity or *Mestizaje* as the solution to cultural narcissism:

Nationalist movements are emerging all around the world, it really troubles me and we are going to have a lot of wars and intolerance. It's happening now and if we bet that way we'll kill off all possibilities of being *mestizos* and probably of existence; we should all be *mestizos*. That's why I chose Claire, the character of my last novel [*Duerme*]. She's a *mestizo* in all senses. She's a European but has a kind of blood that is only Indian, completely Indian. She is a woman but she dresses like a man and maybe she's a man's soul wrapped in a woman's body. She is European but sometimes she dresses and behaves like an Indian, but she never stays in the Indian part, she leaps out of one into the other. . . .She's a perfect metaphorical *mestizo* . . . (in Reid 1995, 148)

Bullosa's vision of the cybermestiza is an inclusive one in which both performativity and material body are in constant flux, and therefore immune to rigid categorization. It is worth noting, however, that at the end of *Duerme* the protagonist Claire is left in a state of suspended animation, unable to realize her potential in the present. Both she and the posthumans of Bullosa's novel in progress are either voices of the future, or indications of the impossibility of communicating that which falls outside the code, the noise or uncoded variety of the cybermestiza. Throughout, an important distinction to bear in mind is that in all of these virtual constructs, the uses of technology are motivated by material, human agents. The projects that are furthered are not those of technology itself, but rather those of very real people of flesh and blood.

In operational terms, the conflation between human reality and technologically mediated virtual reality stems from a certain confusion surrounding the use of the term "reality." This confusion has its origin in the problem of logical typing. The truth is that various realities exist, at various levels of logical typing. Each is a part of the other, but not the same part. A first step toward a resolution of the problem is the establishment of a hierarchical relation, in terms of logical typing, between the various realities. In the case of the relation between the material and the virtual, the answer is quite simple: the material world is the source of the virtual world, and is therefore logically prior to it. Consequently, material reality occupies a higher level than the virtual in the hierarchy of realities. This becomes apparent if we apply what Anthony Wilden has called the Extinction Rule:

> To test for the orientation of a dependent hierarchy, mentally abolish each level (or order) in turn, and note which other level(s), or order(s), will necessarily become extinct if it becomes extinct. (Wilden 1987b, 74)

If we eliminate the virtual world, the material world will carry on pretty much as before, but if we eliminate the material world, the virtual will cease to exist. What often happens, however, is that the relationship between them is inverted, and so an ideal world of pure information, transcendental and infinite, is posited. It is this illusion, from infinite commerce to infinite cognition, that is currently being hawked. This view fails to take into account the fact that material resources, both human and natural, are not infinite, and to treat them as if they were is to dream not knowing one is dreaming. This is not an innocent illusion, for what is consumed in this world of infinite consumption and communication are real material resources. This is simply the latest version in a long line of Modernity's catalogue of infinite products—infinite progress, infinite perfection, and so forth—all created and motivated by competition for scarce resources. In the academy this is most evident in the commoditization of educational content through the use of the new information technologies, the Fordist move to mass produce interchangeable workers through distance learning, virtual classrooms, and proprietary educational software and CD-ROM programs. This move is especially obvious in the automation of foreign language learning, with its highly structured textbooks, web sites, CDs, and software, all designed to eliminate the individual idiosyncracies of both teaching assistant and undergraduate student. The ideal package in this field seeks to mass-produce identical, simulacratic copies of an idealized but nonexistent "native speaker." Like the technology itself, this approach dematerializes not information, but its human context.

The strong critical tendency to define the new combination or convergence between human and machine as something beyond the material—

> The cyborg skips the step of original unity, of identification with nature in the Western sense. . . .The cyborg would not recognize the Garden of Eden; it is not made of mud and cannot dream of returning to dust. (Haraway 1991b, 151)

—is a political move based on the will to power, the power to control through technology, and founded on a rhetorical strategy that attempts to separate the virtual and the material, that is, the social being and the human organism that supports it and is logically prior to it. As noted above, this strategy operates by placing the virtual and the material in an either/or relation of binary opposition, and then inverting their true relationship by privileging the virtual. But there is always a material reality underlying any virtual reality, and any attempt to deny this is, at best, hugely naive. Neither information nor technology is free, and the decisions as to where and when to use technology are made in a social context of finite resources, be it the U.S. educational system or the nondeveloping world. Technology does not possess independent agency, and can neither instaurate itself nor accept blame for its actions. The uses of technology are messages mediated by a Social Imaginary, an Imaginary produced by humans and, at times, susceptible to transformation by them.

The second issue referred to at the beginning of this chapter was the question of the new nonlinear narrative produced by hypermedia. If the book was the realm of the humanist author, and the Text that of the antihumanist author function, *a la* Foucault, then, following Katherine Hayles (1997), we can characterize the hyperspace of the new media as the site, that virtual space where postmodern theory becomes hyper-reality, or as George Landow (1992) puts it in the subtitles to his two volumes on hypertext, the first of which is widely read in translation in the Spanish-speaking world, *"The Convergence of Contemporary Critical Theory and Technology."*[1]

Hayles describes the book as a discrete object produced by a unified author for an isolated reader, an object whose meaning is found within the printed artefact. In contrast, the Text is a semiotic system, produced by and for fragmented subjects, a system whose various meanings are dispersed through the social system of discourse.[2] Although Texts differ in many respects, they nonetheless share the common feature of human agency. In the measure in which writing is mediated by electronic informational systems, however, a new factor enters into the equation: the intelligent machine. In the case of electronic writing, agency is distributed between humans and machines. This new human/machine interface generates a unique form of cognition. Cognition no longer takes place solely within the human organism, but rather is located in the interaction between human and the nonorganic information processing world of the intelligent machine. From this extra-corporeal discursive locus rises the possibility of a new subject, the posthuman subject, and the concomitant notion of a new kind of cognition, one not located solely within the individual, or even exclusively within a social system of discourse, but rather one distributed across the individual, the social, and the electronically mediated virtual. Therefore, if we associate the author of the book with realism, and the author function of the text with anti-realism, then the new form of distributed cognition, the site, can be linked with virtual realism.[3]

The new techno-informatic mediation has, of course, given rise to new theoretical models.[4] As noted briefly in the first chapter, Hayles (1993), in "Virtual Bodies and Flickering Signifiers," underlines two basic distinctions between the Site and previous forms of writing: the relation between body and informatic device; and the form of signification:

> I understand 'human' and 'posthuman' to be historically specific constructions that emerge from different configurations of embodiment, technology, and culture . . . .the posthuman implies a coupling so intense and multifaceted that it is no longer possible to distinguish meaningfully between the biological organism and the informational circuits in which it is enmeshed. Accompanying this change, I have argued, is a corresponding shift in how signification is understood and corporeally experienced. In contrast to Lacanian psycholinguistics, derived from the generative coupling of linguistics and sexuality, flickering signification is the progeny of the fascinating and troubling coupling of language and machine. (111–12)

This new relation between signifier and signified that Hayles calls "flickering signification" is based on the distinction between the relation "presence/absence," a relation associated with the text (and Derrida), and the relation "pattern/randomness," or order/disorder, a relation associated with information, in Shannon and Weaver's sense of the term. In the world of informatics, the signifier is not just an individual marker, but rather a chain of markers, all linked by codes—the lights on the computer screen are linked to magnetic disks through machine language, compiler language, software programs, and so on, all arranged in a hierarchy of coding levels. That which acts as signifier at one level functions as the signified at the next level. Therefore, changing a signifier at one level, often by means of a single command, produces a cascading effect throughout the entire interlinked hierarchy. Thus a single keystroke can change not only a single presence, but also an entire screen pattern. This simple fact becomes quite important when we take into account the fact that the human, or posthuman, is part of this interconnected chain.

A humble example of technologically mediated literature is found on the Navegador Poético (1999) or *Poetic Navigator* web site. Although not strictly Latin American, it originates in Spain, it features some Latin American poets, and is an excellent example of computer mediated Spanish-language literary production. Following the model developed by Stuart Moulthrop's hyperfiction *Hegirascope* (1995), the Poetic Navigator utilizes a software function known as "client pulling" to randomly select lines from poems stored in memory and "pull" these across the computer screen, one after another. The viewer has the option of controlling the speed at which these lines appear and disappear, either faster or slower depending on one's mood, and also of choosing the works, within the limits of those stored in memory, from which the lines of poetry are drawn. According to the site:

> The Poetic Navigator doesn't limit itself to selecting fragments of poems published on the Badajosa EP site, but also, following the practices of the surrealists and the dadaists, mingles fragments amongst themselves to create "exquisite cadavers."

This reference to the avant-garde and modernist tradition recalls the view of hypertext offered by two of its most influential proponents, David Bolter and Michael Joyce, in their 1987 article "Hypertext and Creative Writing," in which they argue hypertext is "a continuation of the modern 'tradition' of experimental literature" (41), logically following "modernism, futurism, Dada surrealism" (44) and so on.

The effect of the Poetic Navigator is to constantly produce new works by means of the intertextual mingling of existing poems. The idea is that all creative works borrow from and reciprocally influence each other through time in a given literary tradition, and what the computer does is to simultaneously speed up this process and make quite clear, transparent if you will, how important and pervasive this intertextual influence is, and so how collective, rather than subjective or objective, our social unconscious really is.

Additionally, the reader is made aware of the futility of reading in the digital world, the world of information overload in which images and words come at us so fast we are overwhelmed, unable to make sense of one before the next is passing us by, all headed for an informational Río Azul. In terms of these goals, the site is quite effective. As to the nature of the poetry so produced, one must keep in mind that to use previous theories of literary criticism to compare the computer-generated output with the originals is doubly to compare apples with oranges, and to miss the point. It must be admitted, however, that the computer production is, at times, vaguely reminiscent of the proverbial million monkeys pounding on a million keyboards.

Another important element in hypermedia is the changed nature of the page itself. The differences between the electronic page and the printed page are many and varied but, in general terms, we can identify three areas of distinction: the visual—graphics, digitalized photos, video, motion, and so forth; the acoustic; and interaction—hyperlinks, e-mail, individualization software applications, and so forth.

As a rule, these features are not found in isolation but in combination with each other.[5] The interactive combination of the visual and the acoustic highlights an important feature of the electronic text, namely the strong tendency toward communicational convergence. What were relatively independent technologies twenty years ago—television, film, telephone, radio, computer—are now inextricably linked in what is known as hypermedia.

The most important distinction of this emergent phenomenon is not simply the fact of the convergence of formerly distinct media, but rather the nonlinear form of this hyperlinking, in marked contrast to the relative lineality of traditional narrative. Since narrative provides important social coding, a change in narrative form can signal concomitant social changes. Hayden White addresses the importance of narrative in socio-cultural coding when he writes:

> to raise the question of the nature of narrative is to invite reflection on the very nature of culture and, possibly, even on the nature of humanity itself. . . .Far from being one code among many that a culture may utilize for endowing experience with meaning, narrative is a metacode, a human universal on the basis of which transcultural messages about the nature of a shared reality can be transmitted. (in Landow 1992, 103–4)

A Latin American example of nonlinear narrative is Uruguayan Ana Sotari's "Cuento inconcluso" ["Unending Story"], an ongoing short story that utilizes hyperlinks to direct the reader to alternate narrative paths. By clicking on highlighted words or "embedded links" within the story, one can go to other pages, and from these to yet others, in such a manner as to be able to avail oneself of various narrative paths toward the provisional end of the constantly evolving—more is added through the course of time—story. This configuration is a version of Eastgate's (www.eastgate.com) classic Storyspace software format, made popular in North America by writers such as Stuart Moulthrop and Michael Joyce. Unfortunately, *Storyspace* software does not accommodate the special characters of languages other than English and so cannot be used by people writing in languages other than English. Consequently, authors seeking to utilize a hypertext format in Spanish, for instance, must construct their own hyperlinks, and the results are often less complex than what those using the prepackaged software are able to achieve. Therefore, although the site offers a glimpse of the possibilities afforded by hypertext, the reader cannot truly produce her own narrative version, and must follow Sotari's narrative. While the hyperlinks offer experimental devices to the reader, these are not qualitatively different from previous avant-garde techniques, and indeed are much less complicated than those found in such works as Julio Cortázar's *Rayuela* (1963), Apollinaire's *Calligrammes* (1916), or Raymond Queneau's *Cent mille milliards de poèmes* (1961).

In terms of the tendency toward communicational convergence noted above, we need to consider how this convergence is affecting the multimedia narrative messages currently being produced in Latin America. What kind of composite images—aural, textual, graphic—are being constructed and what do they say at the message level and, importantly, what do they do at the level of the code?

An exhaustive review of these is impossible, given their sheer number and ephemeral nature, but some sites exhibit certain general characteristics of many of the multimedia writers who operate from within Latin America, and who produce the present-day equivalents of the takes on technology we have followed from *One Hundred Years of Solitude* and *The House of the Spirits*. One such case is the web site entitled *Arbol velóz* (1998), which features the poetry of Luis Bravo. This site, *Swift Tree* in English, takes its name from the traditional relation between trees and paper, and the newer theoretical metaphors of branching, root systems, rhizomes, and so forth associated with the Web and poststructuralist theories of the text. "Velóz" or swift refers to the speed of electronic diffusion and transmission in the new media. The site features a combination or convergence of poetry, sound, graphics, and video, all hyperlinked in various ways. One can read the poems on the screen in English, Spanish, or Portuguese, or one can hear them recited, with or without accompanying video. The site is actually an extended advertisement for a CD-ROM and accompanying book (1998), each featuring a distinct selection of poems by Luis Bravo with the support of twenty Uruguayan musicians, graphic designers, photographers, animators, and technicians. The project bills itself as the first of its kind in Uruguay. One of the artistic goals of the project is to "integrate the oldest forms of creative expression with the most modern techniques of production and distribution" (Bravo 1998). In the introduction, the poet Luis Bravo refers to the origins of poetry "as song, a particular form of integrating sound and image by means of the recited word with the accompaniment of musical instruments," and sees multimedia as a way to recapture this original poetic authenticity, to afford the twentieth-century receptor the opportunity to "connect with the ancestral art of poetry." Again according to Bravo, the multimedia poems of this collection offer the user a chance to re-encounter the original "myths, legends or implicit poetic discourses that, by association, form a dialogue between the poetic tradition of antiquity and that of modernity."

In other words, much as we saw in the case of Walter Lima's film *The Dolphin*, though the form is postmodern, the content is quite Modern, taking us back to our Western cultural origins, the *epos griegos* in Bravo's words. The same can be said of the vast majority of web sites constructed by Latin Americans. Most of these have medial convergence and hyperlinks, but the actual content is generally an impoverished imitation of print, television, video, radio, CD-music, and other existing sources. This is also true of First World web sites, which is not surprising since nearly all use software developed in First World countries. Additionally, the more technologically advanced the software, the greater the need for advanced hardware. The latest browser and Pentium chip are generally minimum requirements to view sites that make extensive use of Java script, digitalized video, audio, and interactive telephony. Even with the correct equipment, a certain degree of technoliteracy is required simply to configure the browser, navigate to the sites, download the plug-ins, and eventually make everything work. This makes the new media hugely elitist, and makes even cyberauthors dependent not only on the hardware and the software, but on the technical support of those who run the servers, and the financial cooperation of the institutions who pay the support staff, and who pay to continually upgrade hardware and software.

There are, of course, pages whose content is supposedly liberatory, counterhegemonic if you will. The Zapatista pages are the most famous example of this (http://www.ezln.org [bilingual]; http://www.spin.com.mx/~floresu/EZLN/ [Spanish only]), but there are many others, generally predicated upon a given minority interest group: racial—African American, Native American; genderic—gay and/or lesbian; ethnic—Hispanic, Bosnian, and so forth. But again, while the form is hypertextual or postmodern, the content is generally modern in that the purported goal of most of these excluded groups is to gain inclusion, to become accepted members of middle- and upper-class postindustrial society, to enjoy the fruits of Modernity. The Social Imaginary itself is not challenged, but rather the hierarchies of privilege within it. The idea is not to change the rules, but simply the players. Just as Arbol velóz rehearses Modernity's originary discourse, these too harken back to that most basic of Greek discourses, Tragedy, the *agonistic* struggle for control of inheritance in its two interwoven threads of bloodline and material resources. Tragedy and Epic are about legitimation, about who will be coded as sacrificial victim and who won't be, about competition and power, about the establishment, not the dissolution, of differences. And so the discourse in much of the new media is a discourse about competition for, and the power to control, human and material resources. It is the discourse of both West and East, mediated by the oppositional metaphysics of the global Social Imaginary.

The technological fallacy that new media and new narrative forms must produce new social coding is, at least up to the present moment, just that. The medium is not the message. The message is what the new media say, and what they do, and in both cases the answer is they reinforce present structures, and even amplify them. This ultimate stage of Latin American narrative, if it can still be called narrative, follows the pattern of previous Latin American narrative. It is mediated by the discourse of technoscience, and searches for a resolution to the question of the impact of the dominating uses of technology in Latin America. What is new is that it now embraces technology rather than rejecting it as foreign and imposed. But in seeing the new media as a new beginning, a story of dematerialized origins without original sin, it repeats the mistake of looking for the arrival of a new destining from without, rather than looking within to a new definition of bienestar that will produce as ultimate social mediation a Social Symbolic capable of generating liberating messages or uses of technology.

8
Conclusion

In the preceding chapters we have seen various ways in which Latin American narrative influences, and is influenced by, the discourses of science and technology. Literary responses to science and technology have ranged from the outright rejection of foreign, dominating technology seen in works such as *The House of the Spirits* and *Like Water for Chocolate* to the exuberant embrace of technology seen in much of the literature produced by means of the new digital media. In what follows I wish to review these diverse perspectives by looking at three representative views of the relations between technoscience and creative production in Latin America: a recent novel by the Costa Rican writer Fernando Contreras Castro, *Los Peor* (1995), which is emblematic of that view which equates science and technology with North American domination; the Brazilian director Carlos Diegues's film *Bye Bye Brazil* (1979), which rehearses a perspective that grudgingly accepts the apparent inevitability of technological change; the radical synthesis of the sciences and the humanities offered by the Cuban-American poet Rafael Catalá's *SciencePoetry* (1986).

Los Peor [*The Worst Family*] combines several of the negative attitudes toward foreign technology seen in works such as *One Hundred Years of Solitude*, *The House of the Spirits*, and *Like Water for Chocolate*. In Contreras Castro's second novel, the central features of this unfavorable rendering are a demonization of science and technology through a portrayal of the evils wrought through multinational agribusiness' massive use and abuse of agrochemicals, a rejection of First World medical science and scientists—in this case a Doctor Evans, a gringo medical doctor—and a concomitant effort to resurrect and privilege indigenous healing practices.

The novel begins with the arrival of a young peasant woman at the brothel which the principal characters in the book call home, and which is in fact a metaphor for the modern consumer world in which everything is for sale. The young woman, six months pregnant and severely ill with gastrointestinal problems, has been forsaken by her family and left on the steps of the modest establishment. Upon learning that the poor woman cannot keep any food down, the owner of the house, Consuelo Peor, calls for Doctor Evans, who in the book represents First World medical science. Evans determines she has been exposed to dangerous agrochemicals in her home province, the agricultural region of Alajuela, which is also Contreras Castro's place of birth.[1] He then prescribes medicines and a diet to follow and leaves. On his way out he bumps into Consuelo's brother, Jeronimo Peor, and briefly outlines the case to him.

Many years earlier, Jeronimo had suddenly disappeared to join a Franciscan monastery somewhere in South America and had finally, after years of wandering, returned to San José and accidentally found his sister Consuelo again. Although he still wears the Franciscan habit he is no longer counted by them as one of their order. Everyone but Consuelo thinks he is crazy, for he spends most of his time walking the streets of San José, carrying an incomprehensible sign and licking the sidewalks. But since he is family, and harmless, Consuelo takes him in and cares for him, as she did for her husband, "yet another nonproductive man" (Contreras Castro 1995, 19). Consuelo's husband, it should be mentioned, is an archetypical victim of technology, one who "worked years without a contract in a factory; they didn't show him how to use the machinery, and one day he received a massive electric shock: cerebral lesions, nothing could be done, and no one took responsibility" (20). His experience with industrial technology, and later medical technology, leaves him a mindless somnambulist.

After Evans leaves, Jeronimo goes to his room and takes some mysterious powders from the wooden boxes in which he had them stored. These he gives to the young woman, who takes them "because she had more faith in the Franciscan habit than the white lab coat" (23). Immediately, and "miraculously," she begins to get better. The author writes:

> It was not in vain that Jeronimo had spent as much time living with the indigenous tribes of South America as he had living with the Franciscans: he had learned to cure with herbs, and since his discovery of the Central Market he had spent countless hours in the herbal shops acquiring a minutely detailed knowledge of each new plant, each leaf, each root, each new type of sap produced by the medicinal plants to which the herbalists, who were quite taken with him, introduced him. (23)

In the end, Jeronimo cures the girl, much to the displeasure of Evans, who "would get furious to find that the girl preferred the 'superstitions of the indians' to the medicine of the pharmacies" (27). Here Contreras Castro privileges "authentic" indigenous knowledge over ratio-scientific knowledge, a move that Latin American writers repeat time and again in the Edenic literature of technoscientific rejection.

Relatedly, it is worth noting that Jeronimo uses all his senses, as opposed to our modern penchant for scopophilia, to observe the world around him, and here the contrast with Evans is made again:

> But he [Jeronimo] didn't only taste the city; he also smelled it and listened to it, and the smell of the hamburger stands disgusted him because, as he used to say, they smelled like Doctor Evans's little black bag. But he loved the odor of the fruit and vegetable stands. (28)

And while the reader might well imagine that Jeronimo is referring only to the fruit and vegetable stands that carry organic produce, the point is the contrast between indigenous holism and modern hyperspecialization.

Although Jeronimo cures the peasant women of her case of pesticide poisoning, he is too late to undo the damage done her unborn child. When the child is born, he suffers from a major pesticide-induced birth defect: he has but one eye, and it is in the center of his forehead. The rest of the novel is dedicated to contrasting the unique views of the supposedly crazy Jeronimo and the "monstrous," one-eyed child named Polifemo with those of modern, ratio-productive society. In one instance of this, Polifemo's cycloptic perspective is contrasted with Evans' insistence on the necessity of a binary viewpoint:

> According to Doctor Evans, the child simply could not survive in a world designed to be seen from the double angle of two eyes . . . and [Evans] continued for a long while to expound upon the necessity of an instrumental binarism in order to perceive the world, and only shut up when an angry Jeronimo finally intervened to refute Evans' theory. (50)

And in the end, Jeronimo is right, because where Evans predicts the child will not survive, Jeronimo's indigenous healing knowledge saves him.

In yet another example of modern, rational science versus mysterious indigenous knowledge, Evans has prescribed a huge number of pills for Consuelo's husband, and Jeronimo gets him off the pills and back to a semblance of normalcy:

the treatments of Jeronimo, that had as their foundation the abandonment of the colored pills that kept him in a state of somnambulism. . . . Jeronimo had managed to lower his dependency to half a pill at lunch and another at dinner. (75)

Indeed, the idea of healing through non-technoscientific means is a leitmotif in the novel. Jeronimo "began with the basic principle that everything was susceptible to being cured" (77), including the city itself, for "it was still possible to return life to that concrete creation" (78). Contreras Castro, utilizing the recurrent motif of the gringo scientist versus indigenous knowledge, extends the idea of a return to a pre-technoscientific world that we have seen in novels such as *The House of the Spirits* and especially in *Like Water for Chocolate*, and specifically offers it as a cure for the ills of modern Latin American society. This view demonizes science and technology—"the Europeans, through their cruel and evil works, depopulated and pillaged the New World, and then filled it with rational men" (105)— but offers no way to usefully incorporate science and technology into Latin American society. In addition to the fact that this view is susceptible to all the same objections levied against it in the chapter treating *Like Water for Chocolate*, the central problem is that nothing short of a nuclear winter will produce a return to a nostalgic, indigenous Eden. Neither technology nor gringos will just go away, and so productive uses must be found for them.

The second perspective, presented in Diegues' film *Bye Bye Brazil* (1979), represents an acceptance of modernization, but a grudging one, which offers various takes on the value of keeping as much as possible of that which is Latin American, while at the same time acknowledging the inevitability of incorporating modern technology into Latin American life. In the words of Diegues, it is about "a country that is beginning to disappear, giving way to one that is just beginning to take form" (in Johnson 1984, 83).

Bye Bye Brazil is a sort of roadshow film, one that depicts the trajectory of Brazilian cinema, Brazilian sociocultural organization, and Brazilian macro- and micro-economic development as these and other elements go through the process of modernization or "multinationalization" in the words of Robert Stam, the move into the twentieth century and beyond.

The film follows the travels of the Caravana Rolidei, a small-time group of circus performers made up of Lorde Cigano (José Wilker), Salomé (Betty Faria), and Andorinha (Príncipe Nabor). Cigano is the leader of the troupe, and doubles as master of ceremonies, magician, clairvoyant, and business manager. Salomé, the sex symbol of the group, performs as an exotic dancer in their show, and also uses her body to generate good will with local politicians and to raise funds in times of need. Andorhinha, who is black and speechless, is the strongman and general roustabout, the working class member of the group.

The film begins with a long shot of an old ferry boat, people, and merchandise in a small northeastern town. As Randal Johnson explains (84), this opening shot is a reminder and citation of the documentary tendency, the critical realism, of the initial phase of Cinema Nova, back in the early sixties. Indeed, at one level the stylistic evolution of the Caravana throughout the film is an allegory of the stylistic evolution of Cinema Novo, as the Caravana, like Cinema Novo itself, is forced to modernize, and prostitute itself, in order to compete with developments in the entertainment industry, at both the technological and geopolitical levels. As Cigano observes, "We have to keep rolling or we will fall off and screw ourselves." Brazilian film must keep pace with developments both in Hollywood and in television, and now presumably with the world wide web, in order to stay viable. Idealism must compromise with the changing times.

As the Caravana rolls into this first stop, the documentary spell is broken by the blaring loudspeakers of the Caravana, producing both pop music and propaganda for the upcoming show. After Cigano drums up a crowd for the night's show, he makes arrangements with the mayor for the necessary political permission, exchanging an interlude with Salomé for political support, an early example of the need for both art and business, including the art and business of cinema, to prostitute themselves in order to survive. In a later stop the Caravana will be thwarted by a local mayor who throws his support behind another medium, namely television, and specifically Sônia Braga in the soap *Dancin' Days*. At issue is the question of political and financial support for the competing interests of television networks such as TV Globo and Brazilian state film enterprises such as Embrafilme, and the concomitant question of market share.

The show itself fares reasonably well at this first stop, successfully promoting its version of utopia to the country rubes. This vision of utopia, embodied by the exotic other Salomé, who speaks Spanish rather than Portuguese while onstage, and including snow in the sertão or badlands to the sound of Bing Crosby's "White Christmas" so fascinates the local accordionist Ciço (Fábio Jr.) that he joins the troop, bringing along his pregnant wife Dasdô (Zaira Zambelli). In addition to those he holds for the starlet Salomé, Ciço also harbors utopian fantasies about the sea, and so to indulge him the troop journeys next to the shore, a move reminiscent of a famous quote in Brazilian cinema, "The *sertão* will become sea, the sea *sertão*" (from Glauber Rocha's *Black God, White Devil* [1964], a film from the first phase of Cinema Novo, one which emphasized social transformation).

It turns out, however, that the utopia of the sea, with its underlying concepts of water, trade, development, jobs, financial success, and so on is now an industrially polluted sea. The Latin American dream of internal migration is over, the big cities now offering not hope but various forms of social pollution, including *favelas*, violence, unemployment, and poverty. The *grandeza* of Brazil's economic miracle is gone. In addition, in the urban areas another kind of pollution threatens the Caravana: the "fishbones." This is Cigano's term for television antennas, and where these exist the audience for the Caravana disappears, seduced by television with which the Caravana cannot compete. Cigano decides the Caravana must return to the small towns of the interior in order to make a living.

In the interior, however, the problem of the Caravana's (Cinema Novo's) struggle with television persists. In a small town Cigano encounters Zé da Luz (Joe of the Light, played by Jofre Soares), who formerly traveled through the interior showing Gilda Abreu's 1946 classic film *O Ebrio* [*The Drunkard*], but who has now been put out of business by the penetration of television into regional cultures. It is in this town that the mayor has opted to support television, opening his own business featuring soap operas. Again, the Caravana must move on.

In a final effort to find a utopia free of television, Cigano decides the Caravana must cross the Amazon to the final frontier, the mythical town of Altamira, where there is such wealth that one has but to pick up precious stones from the ground, and the locals have no place to spend their money. On the way, along the Trans-Amazonian highway, they meet a group of Cruari indians. The local indians, far from being noble savages, are enthralled with things modern and wish more, not less of these. Cigano promptly relieves them of the only authentically Brazilian thing they have, a pet monkey.

When the Caravana arrives in Altamira, they find antennas, jet airplanes, and multinational corporations already exploiting the local resources, both human and natural. In an encounter with representatives of the multinational corporations the Caravana loses everything, and Salomé is forced to prostitute herself to earn enough money to leave Altamira and proceed downriver. In a direct confrontation with multinational technoscience, the old style Caravana (Cinema Novo) is wildly unprepared and nearly wiped out. The only thing that saves the Caravana is the realization that they must prostitute their art to save the business. The days of state-supported critical realism are over. The Caravana/Cinema Novo/Brazil must accept modern values in order to survive and prosper. It is worth noting that after the defeat in Altamira, Andorinha leaves the troop, indicating the fall from grace of the working class in the new era of multinational technology. Andorinha's contribution to the troop was his physical prowess, not his informational expertise, for he did not speak. His departure and perhaps suicide is an indication of the lack of value placed on physical labor in the communication and information age. From now on, the troop will survive by its ability to control goods and services through communication, as Cigano and Ciço enter the modern infotainment age.

The troop now travels back to the big city and its money, and Cigano and Ciço plan to pimp Salomé and Dasdô. Ciço, however, cannot go through with the plan, and refuses to allow Dasdô to participate. He makes one last effort to get Salomé to run off with him but, failing to achieve this utopian fantasy, is forced to leave with Dasdô and their new child, named Altamira, for Brasilia. Cigano and Salomé stay on and, through prostitution and smuggling to the gringos, manage to make their fortune.

"Some time later," as the film tells us, Cigano and Salomé show up in Brasilia to offer Ciço the chance to once again travel with the troop. They now have a new and improved Caravana Rolidey (after an American told Cigano Rolidei was misspelled), a Greyhound bus-type vehicle instead of the old, hand-painted truck they had before. The bus is a rolling bordello, complete with go-go girls, and equipped with all the latest high-tech, modern accessories, from neon lights and stereo sound to television screens on the side. Cigano has gone Hollywood.

In comparison, Ciço, who elects to stay on in Brasilia with his wife and daughter, is playing in a club on the outskirts of Brasilia. In contrast to the disco where he tried, but failed, to pimp Dasdô, he and his group play music with strongly regional elements, and the customers are proletarian, as is their style of dress and dance. They are the workers who came to build the modern, international utopia of Brasilia, and who have been marginalized to the *favelas*, the other Brazil. Ciço's utopia is no longer the fantasy starlet Salomé, nor the "over there" of the sea nor the Amazonian frontier of Altamira, but rather his family and daughter, who is also named Altamira. And although Ciço represents traditional, regional, and rural values, in terms of family, music, dress, dance, and so forth, he does incorporate some of the new. He wears make-up on stage and makes limited use of technology, from the televisions he uses in his act to the very accordion he plays.

It would appear, then, that Diegues offers various possible reactions to the penetration of modern technology into Brazil. Lorde Cigano embraces it heartily, and sees no reason to cling to anything traditional. Ciço, while rejecting its utopian appeal, still finds it useful and indeed necessary. Both Cigano and Ciço use technology to further their own projects, their own value systems, or at least those value systems which serve them. Those who cannot adapt to and incorporate technological innovation into their lives vanish from the scene, as is the case with the workers recruited for the pulp mill in Altamira, Ciço's father, and the strongman Andorinha, all of whom relied on the physical strength and skills characteristic of the industrial revolution and its agropastoral predecessor phases, rather than the information manipulation which characterizes the present digital age.

While Contreras Castro posited modern science and authentic indigenous knowledge as binary opposites, in spite of his critique of Evans's binarism, and Diegues implicitly accepts a fusion of art and technoscientific development, the Cuban-born poet Rafael Catalá, through his Sciencepoetry, makes explicit the notion of synthesis between science and literature:

> The sciences and the humanities, as has already been stated, are subsystems of the sociocultural system. They are integral elements of the fragile and beautiful ecosystem called the Earth. (Catalá 1986, 16)

For Catalá, both the sciences and the humanities, especially literature, are mutually interacting parts of the sociocultural system, a system which is part of a larger structure which contains both society and its environment, the organic and inorganic universe which supports human life. To posit the sciences and the humanities, or technology and art, as antagonistic opposites is to deny society the complete knowledge necessary to integrate system and environment. Catalá writes:

> Sciencepoetry is a practice that upon examination reveals its foundation: a synthesis of two supposedly antagonistic systems: the humanities and the sciences, theory and creation, reason and life—as Unamuno would say. These systems are an expression of knowledge, therefore the opposition doesn't exist. How is it possible that two products of the sociocultural system, whose objective is knowledge of that system, might be perceived as antagonistic entities? (Catalá 1990, 218)

Therefore, for Catalá, Sciencepoetry does not seek to privilege one of the "two cultures" at the expense of the other, but rather seeks to contest the context which forces us to choose between them. Sciencepoetry con-

tests the context of binary competition that has historically sought to justify the exploitation of an environment by a subsystem by converting both
system and environment into pairs of mutually exclusive opposites, such as
man and nature, mind and body, white and non-white, colonizer and colonized, civilized and "primitive," reason and emotion, and the sciences and
the humanities. Catalá (1986) argues instead that the sciences should be
integrated into literary and pedagogical practice, in order to overcome the
current agonistic relation, in which:

> The educational system—at the formal level and at the popular level—exer-
> cises a schismatic function whereby the sciences and the humanities are sepa-
> rated from each other. A child is taught to love one and fear the other. (14)

Catalá takes this notion most directly from the nineteenth-century Cuban intellectual José Martí, whom Catalá credits with inspiring his own
literary and pedagogical theories, citing Martí on literature— "The literature of our times is ineffectual because it doesn't express our era"—and the
educational system—"The divorce between the education one receives in
an era and the era itself is criminal" (in Catalá 1986, 13–15). In other words,
in an age in which technoscientific advances are bringing about the over-
whelming arrival or destining of the competitive project of Modernity, the
evermore complete instauration of the modern world picture, how can it
not be incumbent upon literature to come to grips with technoscientific
reality in a fundamental way, rather than trying to maintain an identity
based on the division between the two cultures. For Catalá, this division is
a false, and indeed self-serving, dichotomy.

By way of illustration of the ecosystemic synthesis that Sciencepoetry
seeks to promulgate both in theory and in practice, let us consider the following poem (Catalá 1986, 37):

My Grandmother and the Ecosystem

Doña Mercedes goes out in the mornings to water
the roots of the cherry tree
The water at the bottom rises towards the leaves
crosses itself and leaps to the sunlit sky
flying towards a cloud.

It sleeps for days on feathery pillows,
and travels for weeks carried in a litter.

> to arrive at the mountains of corn
> and dismounts, a tourist,
> to sample the furrows of these fields.
> Then, it plunges into the depths
> of the earth
> to rest for centuries in an aquifer.

These drops of water have my grandmother for a travel agent.

At one level, this poem describes the water cycle of the earth, a cycle of precipitation and evaporation powered mainly by the energy of the sun and the rotation of the earth. At the inorganic level, the sun-earth system is effectively a closed system. It needs no new input of matter-energy to survive, though, following the second axiom of thermodynamics, it will continue to change as positive entropy builds within the system, most notably in the sun. At the same time, the order of organic nature represented by the grandmother, the cherry tree and the corn does need the input of new matter-energy (and information) to maintain homeostasis, that is, to avoid the disorder predicted by the second axiom of thermodynamics. The relation is one of system (organic nature)/environment. The water in the aquifer is necessary for the survival of the system, not for the survival of the environment. A mistake on the part of the travel agent spells disaster not for the traveler, but for the agent. The relation evoked is not one of competition, but rather one of necessary (from the point of view of the system) cooperation.

This message of synthesis is transmitted not only in the content of the poem but also in the relationship aspect of the poem. By this I mean the relationship between science and literature. A supposedly scientific subject matter, the water cycle of the earth, is given a human face and communicated via a poem. Science and literature converge and perform a synthesizing function rather than a schismatic one. There is no need to "love the one and fear the other" because both are seen as part of the same sociocultural continuum. The relationship aspect of the message is thus congruent with the content aspect of the message. The poem does what it says, if you will.

As a final example, let us look at the following poem (Catalá 1986, 30):

The Humble Neutrino

> The neutrino is blind and deaf,
> very much forgetful,
> to the point where he doesn't see you, and passes right through you

A famous lepton, the neutrino
doesn't feel and ignores the strong force,
it is a son of weak vigor,
and ignores the electromagnetic señora.

It is the most common inhabitant that God made
and that is in turn God

The universe is an ocean of neutrinos
—this omnipresent lord that dominates the gravity of the cosmos.
The rest, float in his waves.

Today it is known that they carry a faint jingle of mass,
and although they are superficially inoffensive,
reader, they pass through you side by side without touching you.

That faint jingle of mass might, one day, obsess the universe
to the point of madness
and cause it to collapse in upon itself.

At one level, this poem exercises the educational function of communicating information regarding subatomic particles in general, and neutrinos in particular: their size, their relative numbers, their interactive characteristics in terms of the four forces (strong, weak, electromagnetic, and gravity), the fact that they are (in the case of neutrons) leptons, and possible ramifications of the big bang theory vis-á-vis the universe, namely, that it may "collapse upon itself" at some future point. At another level, the poem teaches something of the reality of humanity's true relation to the cosmos, to the vastness of inorganic nature which constrains and makes possible organic nature. Also, the poem teaches that science and literature don't have to be mutually exclusive, that we don't have to "love one and hate the other," for both are integrated in this poem. We see science presented in a literary context and, at the same time, literature is presented in such a way that it can be understood in a scientific context. The relationship depicted in the poem is one of integration between the "two cultures," between science and literature.

For Catalá, the division between the sciences and the humanities has its immediate roots in the educational system, in the sense that this division is naturalized and internalized early on by those exposed to the underlying prejudices and presuppositions of our present educational system. The individual then reproduces this false dichotomy automatically, uncritically accepting what has become a subconscious model (Catalá 1998, 544). To illustrate his point Catalá contrasts the cases of two Latin American physicists who turned to creative writing, the Argentine Ernesto Sábato and the Chilean Nicanor Parra. Parra overcame his learned prejudices to incorporate his scientific knowledge into his poetry, while Sábato never surmounted his rejection of science, concluding instead that "The power of science is acquired thanks to a kind of pact with the Devil" (Sábato 1968, 28).

Catalá seems to feel that the demonization of science, as illustrated by Sábato's remark above, can be overcome by education. Essentially, he appears to agree with Ortega that society can change its system of necessities, here defined in terms of educational goals, and in so doing alter societal outcomes, specifically the socioenvironmental problems plaguing Latin America. Catalá (1990) argues that the environmental problems wrought by technology are avoidable if scientific and humanistic thought are integrated, because "The sciences discover the laws that rule the ecosystem. The humanities discover the ethical responsibility of protecting it" (219). To buttress his case, he goes on to document some of the many benefits of science, and to mention a few of the many scientists who have made contributions to humanity, from Pasteur to the Argentine endocrinologist Bernardo Houssay (Nobel Prize 1947). He also reviews the written testimony of some of the numerous scientists who have shared his view on the need for disciplinary integration, including Einstein's *Essays in Humanism*, Erwin Schrödinger's *Science and Humanism*, and J. Robert Oppenheimer's *The Open Mind*, to name but a very few.

Ironically, the very list of like-minded scientists Catalá quotes, and there are many more, stretching back through the centuries, tends to weaken his advocacy of the efficacy of education to change social organization. The notion that the sciences and the humanities are not mutually exclusive is an idea that has been around a long while, but whose time has yet to come. Is this because it is an idea that goes against the grain of Modernity, of the competitive *Ge-stell* of our Social Imaginary? Clearly, this would appear to be the case. Indeed, I would argue that the two discourses, and the relation between them, are necessary structural features of Modernity, features that work together to maintain our current world picture.

The point here, following Rappaport (1969), is to look at what the discourses of the sciences and of the humanities do, rather than what they say, much as the importance of the Tsembaga myths discussed in chapter one resides in what they do, not in what they say. If we look at the discourse of science, we see that one of the things it does is to bring observations of material reality into line with prevailing social constraints. As much recent work in the sociology of scientific knowledge has shown, scientific theory, the stories science tells about its observations, is very much a product of the prevailing social milieu (Haraway 1991b; Harding 1986; Woolgar 1988).

Conversely, humanism begins with socially accepted norms, Catalá's "ethical responsibility," and seeks to make these correspond to the constraints and necessities imposed by the material environment. For example, in a time of diminishing natural resources, the "greening" of the humanities becomes ever more apparent, a greening which, as *Unica* demonstrates, is soon commodified. Likewise, in a period of internationalization of commerce and labor, formerly excluded identities—racial, ethnic, genderic, and so on—become acceptable and even sought after for their exchange value. The discourse of the humanities plays a major role in this expansion. The net effect of these moves is to readjust the balance between system and environment, thus enabling the global society to overcome diacronic obstacles and indeed to prosper not in spite of but because of what were formerly impediments.

Both scientific and humanistic theory function in tandem to govern the relation between society and its material environment. The actions of society change its material environment, which in turn affects society. Additionally, nonsocietally induced changes occur in the material environment, and these too impact society. Again following Rappaport, we can assert that both science and literature produce theories that mediate these relations by producing apparently arbitrary and changing narratives which allow a given society to maintain system-environment relations through time. The claims of nearly all previous theories have been falsified and discredited, yet their product, our present society and the system-environment and class relations that define it, are more alive and well than ever in our current global era. If would seem likely, then, that the use value of a discourse is to be found not in what it says, but in what it does. The cosmology of the Tsembaga says the ancestors must be honored, but the constraints the doing of this imposes on their society—in terms of procreation, agriculture, waste disposal, and warfare—effectively create a homeostatic relation between society and environment. Our modern cosmology—our scientific and humanistic theories—likewise impose constraints that allow continuous growth without, so far, destroying the environment. In both cases, social coding mediates social messages, what people do, so as to avoid extraneous perturbations. The message that is society is protected, by its redundancy or coding, as it passes through time.

As we look back on the various takes on science and technology produced by Latin American narrative, we see that what many of these do is
perpetuate the discourse of Modernity. They may say they are for, against,
or simply neutral with regard to technology, but generally the underlying
message is mediated by the metaphysics of Modernity, from the
demonization of technology seen in novels such as *Like Water for Chocolate*, to the discourse of tragedy in *The Dolphin*, the *epos griego* in *Arbol
velóz*, and the grudging acceptance of technology in *Bye Bye Brazil*. In
other words, much of this narrative is mediated by a now global Social
Imaginary, and what these narratives do is perpetuate that enframing which
is the essence of technology.

If education is to change this, must not it be combined with some mo-
mentous, even cataclysmic change in the material environment, something
"that does not allow itself to be either logically or historically predicted or
to be metaphysically construed as a sequence belonging to a process of
history" (*The Question* 39)? The question concerning the uses of technology is, then, Can Latin American society change its system of necessities
without a wholesale change in the global Social Imaginary, or must it await
the arrival of a new global destining in order to surmount its current
enframing? I would argue that if it can change its social coding, a precondition of such a change is an awareness of the present coding, and that one
source of this awareness can be found in Latin American narrative, if only
we would look.

Notes

INTRODUCTION

1. Throughout, I use the term "Modernity" in its more universal acceptation of the "rationalization" of life, and never to refer to the specifically Spanish American literary movement known as *modernismo*, nor to the distinct Brazilian movement also known as *modernismo*. For a detailed discussion of Spanish American *modernismo* see Jrade (1998), and for Brazilian *modernismo* see Martins (1970).

CHAPTER 1: TAKING RESPONSIBILITY

1. Nietzsche, in *The Birth of Tragedy* (1967), writes: "the influence of Socrates, down to the present moment and even into all future time, has spread over posterity like a shadow that keeps growing in the evening sun" (93), and Friedreich Schlegel proclaims, in *Kritische Friedreich Schlegel Ausgabe* (1: 636), "In this manner, perhaps already Socrates or even farther back, Pythagoras, who first dared to organize morality and the state according to the ideas of pure reason, stand at the apex of modern history, that is, the system of an infinite perfectibility" (in Behler 1991, 20).

2. Weber thought modern society institutionalized instrumental reason in the form of bureaucracy, which in turn transformed instrumental reason into domination. In *Dialectic of Enlightenment* (1987), Horkheimer and Adorno argue that when science enters the cultural field, their term is "the culture industry," the objectifying nature of the scientific epistemology leads to the objectification and domination of human beings.

3. On the distinctions and similarities between Heidegger and Ortega's views on technics and technology, see Mitcham 1994, 39–57; Vatá Menéndez 1961; Fournet-Betancourt 1984.

4. Speaking of adding technology to maintain a given society in a changing (depleting) environment or context, Marvin Harris (1991), in *Cannibals and Kings: The Origins of Cultures*, points out:

> the heart of this process is the tendency to intensify production. Intensification—the investment of more soil, water, minerals, or energy per unit of time or area—is in turn a recurrent response to threats against living standards . . . intensification is always counterproductive . . . it leads inevitably to the depletion of the environment. (5)

5. The list of theoretical portends could include not only Derrida & Co. but also Bajtín's polyphonic novel, and many reader response theorists, including Iser and Fish. For a review of these, see Paternain Miranda. There are also literary antecedents of hypertext, including, for example, Cortázar's *Rayuela*, Pavic's *Diccionario de los Kasarz*, and especially Borges's various labyrinths.

6. The other three are "that which separates the celestial from the terrestrial; the animal from the divine; the rational from the irrational" (Piscitelli 1995, 36), *a la* Copernicus, Freud, and Darwin.

7. Specific information on these and other areas of cyber development can be found in Romero Castillo, Gutiérrez Carbajo, and García Page 1997; Bettetini and Colombo 1995; Trejo 1996; Terceiro 1996; and Landow 1992; 1997.

CHAPTER 2: CONSTRUCTING TECHNOLOGY IN LATIN AMERICAN LITERATURE

1. For a picture of the harbor and town, see the Ilhéus web page at www.bitsnet.com. br/ilheus.html. Amado was born in 1912 in Ilhéus, which is the provincial capital of the state of Bahía, Brazil.

CHAPTER 3: THE TECHNOLOGICAL OTHER

1. For example, the lack of adequate environmental regulations and governmental oversight is an invitation to disaster in fields such as biogenetics and nuclear power, either by accident or by military intention.

2. This growing realization has engendered a new field, cyborg studies:

Cyborg anthropology explores a new alternative by examining the argument that human subjects and subjectivity are crucially as much a function of machines, machine relations, and information transfers as they are machine producers and operators. (Downey, Dumit, and Williams 1995, 343)

3. Throughout, unless otherwise noted, all translations are mine.

4. The image of the gringo scientist is a recurrent one in Latin American literature— Mr. Herbert of the banana company in *One Hundred Years of Solitude* and the "tiny gringo" expert Mr. Brown in *The House of the Spirits* being but two examples. Indeed, from Faust, to Victor Frankenstein and Dr. Strangelove, the scientist is a recurrent theme in Western literature (Haynes 1994). For examples in peninsular literature, see Cano Ballesta (1981).

5. A few examples provided by González Echevarría (1990, 14–15) will serve to illustrate the point: Miguel Angel Asturias (*Leyendas de Guatemala*), Alejo Carpentier (*Los pasos perdidos, ¡Ecué-Yamba-O!*), and Lydia Cabrera (*El monte*), later a student of Fernando Ortiz, all studied ethnology in Paris in the 1930s. Severo Sarduy (*De donde son los cantantes*) was a student of Roger Bastide and, as mentioned previously, José María Arguedas (*Los ríos profundos*) and Miguel Barnet (*Biografía de un cimarrón*) were anthropologists.

6. On the question of whether the novel represents a parodic discourse of resistance to the patriarchal masculine novel, "the revindication of a feminine space" (Chaverri 1992, 31), or is "simplistic, Manichaean, plagued by banal conventionalisms" (Marquet 1991, 58), the admittedly partial review of the literature I have done seems to indicate a bicameral division along feminist/nonfeminist lines. That is, read from a feminist context (Chaverri

1992; Jaffe 1993; Oropesa 1992; González Stephan 1992; Potvin 1995) it is a parody and hence a discourse of resistance, while from the nonfeminist perspective (Marquet 1991; Fadanelli 1990) it is simply clichè. This chapter seeks not to resolve this debate, but rather to address the somewhat more pragmatic issue of the efficacy of the epistemological and ideological positions advocated in the novel, call them what one may, in terms of providing a model for long-term sustainable relations between technoscience, society, and nature in Latin America.

7. On the metadiscourse in anthropology, see Geertz 1983 and Clifford 1988. On the metadiscourse in Latin American narrative, see González Echevarría 1990, 152–53. The best critique of the ethnography of the period, and of Lévi-Strauss, is still Derrida's "The Violence of the Letter: From Lévi-Strauss to Rousseau" (1976, 101–40).

8. For a sampling of the many texts in this field, see Rose on geography (1993); Harding on general science (1986); Haraway on primatology (1991a); Bleier on biology (1984); Mires on ecology (1990); and Wood on cartography (1992).

9. The allusion is to Freud's book of the same name. In English the title is *Civilization and its Discontents*.

10. The film is extremely faithful to the novel (Potvin 1995).

CHAPTER 4: ECOSCIENCE AND ECOTRAVELERS IN THE DISPOSABLE WORLD

1. Latin America is observed through the gaze of the ecotraveler in a whole host of new "eco-visions": Deep Ecology, Ecofeminism, Radical Ecology, Social Ecology, Social Ecofeminism, and so on. For a critique of some of these movements, see Biehl 1991. For an overview, see Zimmerman 1994.

2. According to the San José, Costa Rica newspaper *La República*, (21 Aug. 1994) the novel has recently been produced as a play: "his novel *Unica mirando al mar* that, rapidly, arrived on the stage of the Theater Melico Salazar" (Hernández 1994, 2). I personally saw another version entitled "Unica y la entropía" ["Unica and Entropy"] which was performed in Contreras Castro's hometown of San Ramón in February 1996.

3. On pharmaceuticals, agrochemicals, and plagacides which have been banned in the countries of origin and "dumped" in "underdeveloped" nations, see Sánchez 1992; Simmons 1989; and Donaldson 1989.

4. Contreras Castro, in an interview with Edin Hernández (1994), says "Unica is a character that reflects the archetypical character of the Latin American woman: to be strong, to be steadfast in struggling to continue living" (2).

5. Contreras Castro actually visited the dump as part of his fieldwork for the novel: "I tried to go more than once but I couldn't, the smell is unbearable" (Villalobos 1994, 15).

6. On the social context and construction of Mead's work, see Freeman 1983.

7. For an account of the Mexico City dump, see Guillermoprieto 1990.

8. On bureaucratic-authoritarian regimes, see O'Donnell 1979; and Malloy 1977.

9. North American communications science and technology would seem to have solved the problem of where to put the garbage with the introduction of cable, satellite, fiber optic, and so on. The garbage just vanishes off into the ozone. The problem is, they have to sell a lot of Buicks and Pampers to justify their investment, and these don't vanish as readily.

10. Trapped within the consumer discourse, the discourse of ecology becomes a commodity. Ecoreserves and ecotourism in developing countries have engendered ecodisasters as thousands of unemployed people looking for jobs have overwhelmed the reserves, poaching the wildlife for food, burning the trees for fuel, and polluting the water with their waste

products. See Honey (1994) on Galapagos and Monteverde (Costa Rica); and Mora Castellano (1994) on Costa Rica.

11. On appropriate technologies, see Peña 1992; and Alfaro 1993, 210–12.

12. On the role of scientific discourse in the invention of popular traditions or culture by the very anthropologists and ethnographers who study them, see Hobsbawn and Ranger 1983; Kuper 1988; Linnekin 1992; and Neumann 1992.

13. The title of a chapter in *Crepúsculo de los ídolos* [*Twilight of the Gods*].

CHAPTER 5: POSTMODERN TRANSCULTURATION

1. This view is hardly passé. In a 1995 interview, the Mexican writer Carmen Bullosa states "I think that *Mestizaje* is the best option we all could have.... Nationalist movements are emerging all around the world... and we are going to have a lot of wars and intolerance ... we should all be *mestizos*" (in Reid 1995, 147–48).

2. Around 1897 Unamuno (1966–71) suffered a spiritual crisis after which he turned from his earlier advocacy of the Europeanization of Spain, in works such as "En torno al castecismo," to a rejection of positivist reason, logic, and science in favor of a return to a premodern *volksgeist* in, for example, *Sobre la europeización,* in which Unamuno declares "Hay que africanizarse a la antigua."

3. In *Gödel, Escher, Bach* (1989), Douglas Hofstadter explains:

The "Strange Loop" phenomenon occurs whenever, by moving upwards (or downwards) through the levels of some hierarchical system, we unexpectedly find ourselves right back where we started. (10)

CHAPTER 6: POSTMODERN VISUAL NARRATIVE

1. Dolphins do drive fish from an area, rounding them up with scout dolphins who chase them from the shallows near the beach to the waiting pack members (Ellis 1982, 8–9; Bel'Kovich 1991, 42–43).

2. In "La Pharmacie de Platon" Jacques Derrida (1968) shows how philosophy, from Plato to Nietzsche (who took a contrary stand), has attempted to establish an absolute difference between the two meanings of *pharmakon*—"poison" and "remedy"—when in fact both meanings serve to designate the scapegoat, and so difference is ultimately undermined by symmetry.

3. I am referring here to the myth of Iphegenia and not specifically to Euripides' posthumously produced play *Iphegenia in Aulis*, though the parallels are striking.

4. Gianni Vattimo, in *The Transparent Society* (1992, 28–44) develops this view in great detail. Here I follow his meditations.

5. *Cinema Novo* or New Cinema refers to the films made by young Brazilian cineastes such as Carlos Diegues, Joaquim Pedro de Andrade, and Walter Lima from the early 1960s to approximately 1972. In very general terms, *Cinema Novo* was a movement against commercial or Hollywood films and the values these represented. *Cinema Novo* specifically addressed many of the social and artistic issues assiduously avoided by mainstream film.

6. John King (1990), in *Magical Reels*, explains:

Cannibalism refers back to the Modernist movement of the 1920s culture when ... Oswald de Andrade posed the provocative "Tupy or not Tupy, that is the question" as part of his anthropophagous manifesto. Cannibalism is a form of wilful cultural nationalism, suggesting that the products of the first world can be digested and recycled by the colonized, as a way of countering economic, social, and cultural imperialism. (113)

Products of the first world would include, presumably, their myths.

7. The notion of myth as language reaches its apogee in Claude Lévi-Strauss's *Anthropologie Structurale* (1963) which contains his study of Oedipus. For a review of major trends in the study of myth, and especially Greek myth, see Jean-Pierre Vernant 1990, 203–60.

8. If the Freudian approach proclaims myths to be the symptomatic expression of "lower" unconscious desires, an alternative position, as with Mircea Eliade and Jung, would have it that myth is the expression of something "higher" beyond human understanding: the absolute, totality, the sacred.

9. Bronislaw Malinowski (1922) in *Argonauts of the Western Pacific* points out the gap between interpretations of a symbolist kind and the role myths actually play in societies in which they have stayed alive. Malinowski argues the role myth plays in a living society is very much different from that of bearer of eternal metaphysical truth assigned it in the symbolist interpretive field.

10. I am not unaware that Slater might well object that my reading is hardly de-privileged.

11. Márcio Souza's *A resistível ascenção do Boto Tucuxi* (1982) portrays the *boto* as another type of outsider, this time from the capital. In the book Souza satirizes the power hungry politician Gilberto Mestrinho who, in real life, later recaptured the governorship of Amazonas (1990) by taking the dolphin as his trademark.

12. In *The Predicament of Culture*, James Clifford (1988) describes the field worker–theorist approach:

In the 1920's, the new field worker–theorist brought to completion a new powerful scientific and literary genre, the ethnography, a synthetic cultural description based on participant observation [which] may be briefly summarized as follows . . . First, the persona of the field worker was validated, both publicly and professionally. In the popular domain, visible figures like Malinowski, Mead, and Griaule communicated a vision of ethnography as both scientifically demanding and heroic, . . . the field worker was to live in the native village, use the vernacular, stay a sufficient (but seldom specified) length of time . . . the new ethnographer tended to focus thematically on particular institutions. . . . In the primarily synechdochic rhetorical stance of the new ethnography, parts were assumed to be microcosms or analogies of wholes. (29–31)

13. According to González Echevarría (1990, 153), examples of this metadiscourse in Latin American literature include works such as Augusto Roa Bastos's *Yo el Supremo* and Julio Cortázar's *Rayuela*.

14. Specifically, Nietzsche's position after *The Birth of Tragedy* (1967), beginning with *Human All Too Human* (1986).

CHAPTER 7: THE ARRIVAL OF THE POSTHUMAN

1. Compare Heidegger's Turning with, for example, Foucault's prediction, *avant la lettre electronic*, of a media Turning:

I think that, as our society changes, at the very moment when it is in the process of changing, the author function will disappear, and in such a manner that fiction and its polysemous texts will once again function according to another mode, but still with a system of constraint—one which will no longer be the author, but which will have to be determined or, perhaps, experienced. (Foucault 1979, 160)

2. In "From Work to Text," Barthes (1971) explains the irreducible plurality of the Text:

> The Text . . . practices the infinite deferment of the signified . . . it is structured, but off-centred, without closure . . . it accomplishes the very plurality of meaning: an *irreducible* . . . plural. (155)

3. Scott Bukatman (1993), taking as his point of departure Ernest Mandel's concept of the "long waves" of capitalism, an idea later developed by Fredric Jameson, describes this evolution in terms of the technologies of each period: "Machine, Nuclear, and Information Ages . . . electronic follows nuclear which followed mechanical" (5).

4. See, for example, George P. Landow's (1992; 1997), *Hypertext: The Convergence of Contemporary Critical Theory and Technology* (or his more recent release, *Hypertext 2.0*), or, for a less hyperutopic view, see Espen Aarseth's (1997) excellent *Cybertext: Perspectives on Ergodic Literature*. In Spanish, Alejandro Piscitelli's (1995) *Ciberculturas: En la era de las máquinas inteligentes* [*Cybercultures: In the Age of Intelligent Machines*] is outstanding.

5. For a detailed description of these distinctions, see Ziegfeld (1989).

CHAPTER 8: CONCLUSION

1. In an interview with Contreras Castro, in February of 1997 in San José, Costa Rica, he told me that the incidents of agrochemical abuses, poisonings, birth defects, and so on in the book are based upon actual incidents that have happened, and still happen, in Costa Rica. He blames these on multinational agribusiness interests.

Bibliography

Aarseth, Espen J. 1997. *Cybertext: Perspectives on Ergodic Literature*. Baltimore: Johns Hopkins University Press.

Alfaro, Mario C. 1993. "La tecnología: Algunos de sus calificativos y enfoques." In *Dédalo y su estirpe: Historia-tecnología-filosofía*, edited by Alvaro Zamora and Mario Alfaro, 209–20. Cartago, Costa Rica: Editorial tecnológica de Costa Rica.

Allende, Isabel. 1986. *The House of the Spirits*. Translated by Magda Bogin. New York: Bantam.

Amado, Jorge. 1974. *Gabriela, Clove and Cinnamon*. New York: Avon.

Arbol velóz. Online. Internet. Available http://www.chasque.apc.org/rusinek/

Badosa EP. Online. Internet. Available http://www.cccbxaman.org/badosa.

Barthes, Roland. 1971. "From Work to Text." In *Image, Music, Text*, edited and translated by S. Heath, 155–64. París: Editions du Seuil.

Bastos, María Inês, and Charles Cooper, eds. 1995. *Politics of Technology Policy in Latin America*. New York: Routledge.

Bateson, Gregory. 1989. *Steps to an Ecology of Mind: Collected Essays in Anthropology, Psychiatry, Evolution, and Epistemology*. New York: Ballantine.

Baudrillard, Jean. 1983. *Simulations*. Translated by Paul Foss et al. New York: Semiotext(e).

Behler, Ernst. 1991. "Problems of Origin in Modern Literary History." In *Theoretical Issues in Literary History*, edited by David Perkins, 9–34. Cambridge, MA and London: Harvard University Press.

Bel'Kovich, V. M. 1991. "Herd Structure, Hunting, and Play: Bottlenose Dolphins in the Black Sea." In *Dolphin Societies: Discoveries and Puzzles*, edited by Karen Pryor and Kenneth S. Norris, 17–78. Berkeley: University of California Press.

Benítez Rojo, Antonio. 1989. *La isla que se repite: El caribe y la perspectiva posmoderna*. Hanover, NH: Ediciones del Norte.

Bettetini, Gianfranco, and Fausto Colombo, eds. 1995. *Las nuevas tecnologías de la comunicación*. Translated by J. C. Gentile Vitale. Barcelona: Paidós.

Biehl, Janet. 1991. *Rethinking Ecofeminist Politics*. Boston: South End Press.

Bleier, Ruth. 1984. *Science and Gender: A Critique of Biology and its Theories of Women*. New York: Pergamon.

Bolter, David, and Michael Joyce. 1987. "Hypertext and Creative Writing." In *Hypertext '87: Proceedings*, 41–50. New York: Association for Computing Machinery.

Bopp, Raul. N.d. *Cobra Norato e outros poemas*. Rio de Janeiro: Civilização Brasileira.

Bravo, Luis. 1998. *Arbol Veloz: Poemas 1990–1998*. Montevideo: Ediciones Trilce.

———. 1998. *Arbol Veloz: Poemas 1990–1998*. CD-ROM. Montevideo: Ediciones Trilce.

Bukatman, Scott. 1993. *Terminal Identity: The Virtual Subject in Postmodern Science Fiction*. Durham, NC: Duke University Press.

Bushnell, Rebecca. 1988. *Prophesying Tragedy: Sign and Voice in Sophocles' Theban Plays*. Cornell: Cornell University Press.

Bye Bye Brazil. 1979. Directed by Carlos Diegues. New Yorker Films.

Cano Ballesta, Juan. 1991. *Literatura y tecnología: Las letras españolas ante la revolución industrial: 1900–1933*. Madrid: Orígenes.

Case, Sue-Ellen. 1985. "Classic Drag: The Greek Creation of Female Parts." *Theater Journal* 37, no. 3: 317–27.

———. 1995. "Performing Lesbian in the Space of Technology: Part II." *Theatre Journal* 47: 329–43.

Castoriadis, Cornelius. 1987. *The Imaginary Institution of Society*. Translated by Kathleen Blamey. Cambridge, MA: MIT Press.

Catalá, Rafael. 1986. *Cienciapoesía*. Minneapolis: Prisma.

———. 1990. "Para una teoría latinoamericana de las relaciones de la ciencia con la literatura: La cienciapoesía." *Revista filosofía* 28, no. 67–68: 215–23.

———. 1998. "Literatura y ciencia en las culturas de habla española." *La Torre* 3, no. 9: 529–50.

Chaverri, Amalia. 1992. "*Como agua para chocolate:* Transgresión de límites/Reivindicación de espacios." *Sociocriticism* 8, no. 1: 7–35.

Clifford, James. 1988. *The Predicament of Culture: Twentieth-Century Ethnography, Literature, and Art*. Cambridge: Harvard University Press.

Conniff, Brian. 1990. "The Dark Side of Magical Realism: Science, Oppression, and Apocalypse in *One Hundred Years of Solitude*." *Modern Fiction Studies* 36, no. 2: 167–79.

Contreras Castro, Fernando. 1993. *Unica mirando al mar*. San José, Costa Rica: ABC.

———. 1997. Personal Interview. 15 February.

———. 1995. *Los Peor*. San José, Costa Rica: Ediciones Farben.

Derrida, Jacques. 1968. "La Phamarcie de Platon." In *La Dissémination*, 71–179. Paris: Seuil.

———. 1976. *Of Grammatology*. Translated by G. Spivak. Baltimore: Johns Hopkins University Press.

Dery, Mark. 1993. "Flame Wars." *South Atlantic Quarterly* 92, no. 4: 559–68.

Diccionario Porrúa. 1985. Mexico City: Porrúa.

Donaldson, Thomas. 1989. "Moral Minimums for Multinationals." *Ethics and International Affairs* 3: 163–82.

Downey, Gary Lee, Joseph Dumit, and Sarah Williams. 1995. "Cyborg Anthropology." In *The Cyborg Handbook*, edited by Chris Hables Gray, 341–46. New York: Routledge.

Elias, Thomas D. 1994. "The Miracle Worker. How Alfonso Arau's 'Water for Chocolate' Dream Came True." *Chicago Tribune* 6 March, sec. 13: 19.

Ellis, Richard. 1982. *Dolphins and Porpoises.* New York: Knopf.

Esquivel, Laura. 1990. *Como agua para chocolate: Novela de entregas mensuales con recetas, amores y remedios caseros.* Mexico: Planeta.

Fadanelli, Guillermo J. 1990. "Literatura a la que estamos condenados/I. Laura Esquivel. La literatura del huevo tibio." *Unomasuno* 873: 4.

Flieger, Jerry Aline. 1983. "The Purloined Punchline: Joke as Textual Paradigm." *MLN* 98 no. 5: 941–67.

Fortes, Jacqueline, and Larissa Adler Lomnitz. 1994. *Becoming a Scientist in Mexico: The Challenge of Creating a Scientific Community in an Underdeveloped Country.* Translated by Alan P. Hynds. University Park: Pennsylvania State University Press.

Foster, David William. 1983. *Para una lectura semiótica del ensayo latinoamericano: Textos representivos.* Madrid: Porrúa.

Foucault, Michel. 1973. *The Order of Things: An Archaeology of the Human Sciences.* New York: Vintage.

———. 1979. "What is an Author?" In *Textual Strategies: Perspectives in Post-Structuralist Criticism.* Translated and edited by Josué V. Harari, 141–60. Ithaca: Cornell University Press.

Fournet-Betancourt, Raúl. 1984. "Dos aproximaciones filosóficas al problema de la técnica: Ortega y Heidegger." *Cuadernos Hispanoamericanos* 2.29–30: 200–235.

Freeman, Derek. 1983. *Margaret Mead and Samoa: The Making and Unmaking of an Anthropological Myth.* Cambridge: Harvard University Press.

Freud, Sigmund. 1984. *El malestar en la cultura.* Translated by Ramón Rey Ardid. México: Alianza.

Fuss, Diana. 1989. *Essentially Speaking.* New York and London: Routledge.

García Márquez, Gabriel. 1971. *One Hundred Years of Solitude.* Translated by Gregory Rabassa. New York: Bard.

García Canclini, Néstor. 1989. *Culturas híbridas: Estrategias para entrar y salir de la modernidad.* Mexico: Grijalbo.

———. 1995. *Consumidores y ciudadanos: Conflictos multiculturales de la globalización.* Mexico: Grijalbo.

Geertz, Clifford. 1988. *Works and Lives: The Anthropologist as Author.* Stanford: Stanford University Press.

Girard, René. 1977. *Violence and the Sacred.* Translated by Patrick Gregory. Baltimore and London: Johns Hopkins University Press.

González Echevarría, Roberto. 1990. *Myth and Archive: A Theory of Latin American Literature.* New York: Cambridge University Press.

González Stephan, Beatriz. 1992. "Para comerte mejor: Cultura calibanesca y formas literarias alternativas." *Nuevo texto crítico* 5, no. 9/10: 201–15.

Guillermoprieto, Alma. 1990. "Letter from Mexico City." *The New Yorker.* 17 September: 93–96.

Haraway, Donna J. 1991a. *Primate Visions: Gender, Race and Nature in the World of Modern Science.* New York: Routledge.

———. 1991b. *Simians, Cyborgs, and Women: The Reinvention of Nature.* London: Free Association Books.

Harding, Sandra. 1986. *The Science Question in Feminism.* Ithaca and London: Cornell University Press.

Harris, Marvin. 1991. *Cannibals and Kings: The Origins of Cultures.* New York: Vintage.

Hayes, Roslynn D. 1994. *From Faust to Strangelove: Representations of the Scientist in Western Literature.* Baltimore and London: Johns Hopkins University Press.

Hayles, Katherine L. 1993. "Virtual Bodies and Flickering Signifiers." October 66: 69–91.

———. 1995. "The Life Cycle of Cyborgs: Writing the Posthuman." In *The Cyborg Handbook,* edited by Chris Hables Gray, 321–35. New York and London: Routledge.

———. 1997. "Opening Address." Seminar: Narrating Virtuality: Genderflexing, Infoworlds, and Posthumans. Morgantown, WV, 5 June.

Heidegger, Martin. 1977. *The Question Concerning Technology and Other Essays.* Translated by William Lovitt. New York: Harper.

———. 1983. "El principio de razón." In *¿Qué es filosofía?*, translated by José Luis Molinuevo, 69–93. Madrid: Narcea.

Hernández, Edin. 1994. "*Unica*: La forteleza de la desesperación." *Signos: Semanario cultural.* 36 Aug.: 1–2.

Hernández-Boada, Gustavo. 1995. "Colombia and the Challenge of Biotechnology." In *Biotechnology in Latin America: Politics, Impacts, and Risks,* edited by N. Patrick Peritore and Ana Karina Galve-Peritore, 127–36. Wilmington, DE: SR Books.

Hobsbawm, Eric and Terence Ranger, ed. 1983. *The Invention of Tradition.* Cambridge: Cambridge University Press.

Hofstadter, Douglas R. 1989. *Gödel, Escher, Bach: An Eternal Golden Braid.* New York: Vintage Books.

Honey, Martha. 1994. "El precio del ecoturismo." *Américas.* 46, no. 6 Washington, D.C.: OEA: 40–47.

Horkheimer, Max, and Theodor Adorno. 1987. *The Dialectic of Enlightenment.* New York: Continuum.

Ihde, Don. 1983. "The Historical-Ontological Priority of Technology over Science." *Philosophy and Technology,* edited by Paul T. Durbin, 235–52. Dordrecht: Reidel.

Jaffe, Janice. 1993. "Hispanic American Women Writer's Novel Recipes and Laura Esquivel's *Como agua para chocolate.*" *Women's Studies* 22: 217–30.

Johnson, Randal. 1984. *Cinema Novo x 5.* Austin: University of Texas Press.

Johnson, Randal, and Robert Stam, eds. 1995. *Brazilian Cinema.* New York: Columbia University Press.

Jrade, Cathy L. 1998. *Modernismo, Modernity, and the Development of the Spanish American Novel.* Austin: University of Texas Press.

King, John. 1990. *Magical Reels: A History of Cinema in Latin America.* London: Verso.

Kuper, Adam. 1988. *The Invention of Primitive Society.* London: Routledge.

Lacan, Jacques. 1968a. "The Function of Language in Psychoanalysis." In *The Language of the Self*, edited by A. Wilden. Baltimore: Johns Hopkins University Press.

———. 1968b. "The Mirror-Phase." Translated by Jean Roussel. *New Left Review* 51: 71–7.

Landow, George P. 1992. *Hypertext: The Convergence of Contemporary Critical Theory and Technology.* Baltimore: Johns Hopkins University Press.

———. 1997. *Hypertext 2.0: The Convergence of Contemporary Critical Theory and Technology.* Baltimore: Johns Hopkins University Press.

Latour, Bruno, and Steve Woolgar. 1979. *Laboratory Life: The Social Construction of Scientific Facts.* Beverly Hills, CA: Sage.

Lerner, Gerta. 1986. *The Creation of Patriarchy.* New York: Oxford University Press.

Lévi-Strauss, Claude. 1963. *Structural Anthropology.* Translated by C. Jacobson and B. G. Schoepf. Garden City, NY: Anchor.

———. 1992 (1955). *Tristes tropiques.* Translated by John and Doreen Weightman. New York: Penguin.

Lima, Robert. 1995. *Dark Prisms: Occultism in Hispanic Drama.* Lexington: University Press of Kentucky.

Linnekin, Jocelyn. 1992. "On the Theory and Politics of Cultural Construction in the Pacific." *Oceania* 62: 249–63.

Lyotard, Jean-Francois. 1984. *The Postmodern Condition: A Report on Knowledge.* Translated by Geoff Bennington and Brian Massumi. Minneapolis: University of Minnesota Press.

Malinowski, Bronislaw. 1922. *Argonauts of the Western Pacific.* New York: Dutton.

———. 1991. "Fernando Ortiz." *Historia y crítica de la literatura hispanoamericana.* Vol. 2. Edited by Cedomil Goic. Barcelona: Crítica.

Malloy, James M., ed. 1977. *Authoritarianism and Corporatism in Latin America.* Pittsburgh: University of Pittsburgh Press.

Marquet, Antonio. 1991. "¿Cómo escribir un best seller? La receta de Laura Esquivel." *Plural* 237: 58–67.

Martine, George, and Claudio Castro. 1985. *Biotecnología e sociedade: O caso brasileiro.* Campinas, Brazil: N.p.

Martins, Wilson. 1970. *The Modernist Idea: A Critical Survey of Brazilian Writing in the Twentieth Century.* Translated by Jack E. Tomlins. New York: New York University Press.

McClintock, Anne. 1995. *Imperial Leather: Race, Gender, and Sexuality in the Colonial Contest.* New York and London: Routledge.

Merrell, Floyd. 1974. "José Buendía's Scientific Paradigms: Man in Search of Himself." *Latin American Literary Review* 2, no. 4: 59–70.

Mires, Fernando. 1990. *El discurso de la naturaleza: ecología y política en América Latina,* San José, Costa Rica: DEI.

Mitcham, Carl. 1994. *Thinking Through Technology: The Path Between Engineering and Philosophy.* Chicago: University of Chicago Press.

Moore, Omar Khayyam. 1969. "Divination—A New Perspective." In *Environment and Cultural Behavior: Ecological Studies in Cultural Anthropology,* edited by Andrew Vayda, 121–29. Garden City: Natural History Press.

Mora Castellano, Eduardo. 1994. "El ecoturismo costarricense es un simple turismo con muy mal eco." *Ambien-tico.* No. 19, San José: Universidad Nacional: 6–9.

Navegador Poético. 1999. Online. Internet. Available http://www.cccbxaman.org/badosa/np.htm

Navegante. 1999. Online. Internet. Available http://naveg.fcaglp.unlp.edu.ar/guia/guia.html

Neumann, Klaus. 1992. *Not the Way It Really Was: Constructing the Tolai Past.* Honolulu: University of Hawaii Press.

Nietzsche, Friedrich. 1967. *The Birth of Tragedy and The Case of Wagner.* Translated by Walter Kaufmann. New York: Vintage.

———. 1974. *The Gay Science*. Translated by Walter Kaufmann. New York: Random.

———. 1986. *Human All Too Human: A Book For Free Spirits*. Translated by R.D. Hollingdale. Cambridge: Cambridge University Press.

O'Donnell, Guillermo. 1979. *Modernism and Bureaucratic-Authoritarianism: Studies in South American Politics*. Berkeley: University of California Press.

Olien, Michael D. 1973. *Latin Americans: Contemporary Peoples and Their Cultural Traditions*. New York: Holt.

Oropesa, Salvador. 1992. "*Como agua para chocolate* de Laura Esquivel como lectura de *Manual de urbanidad y buenas costumbres* de Manuel Antonio Carreño." *Monographic Review/Revista monográfica* 8: 252–60.

Ortega y Gasset, José. 1945–47a. "El mito del hombre allende de la técnica." *Obras completas*. Madrid: Revista de Occidente, 9. 617–24.

———. 1945–47b. "Meditación de la técnica." *Obras completas*. Madrid: Revista de Occident. 1st ed., 5. 317–75.

Ortiz, Fernando. 1947. *Cuban Counterpoint: Tobacco and Sugar*. Translated by Harriet de Onís. New York: Knopf.

Paternain Miranda, Beatriz. 1997. "Teorías que avalan el concepto de autor en el hipertexto." In *Literatura y multimedia*, edited by José Romero Castillo, Francisco Gutiérrez Carbajo, and Mario García-Page, 297–302. Madrid: Visor Libros.

Peña, Margarita M. 1992. "New Technologies and an Old Debate." In *New Worlds, New Technologies, New Issues*, edited by Stephen H. Cutcliffe, et al., 117–31. Bethlehem: Lehigh University Press.

Piscitelli, Alejandro. 1995. *Ciberculturas: En la era de las máquinas inteligentes*. Buenos Aires: Paidós.

Potvin, Claudine. 1995. "*Como agua para chocolate*: ¿parodia o cliche?" *Revista Canadiense de Estudios Hispánicos* 20, no. 1: 55–67.

Prigogine, Ilya and Isabelle Stengers. 1984. *Order Out of Chaos: Man's New Dialogue With Nature*. New York: Bantam.

Rama, Angel. 1989. *Transculturación narrativa en América Latina*. Montevideo: Fundación Angel Rama.

Rappaport, Roy A. 1969. *Pigs for the Ancestors*. New Haven, CT: Yale Paperbacks.

Reid, Anna. 1995. Interview with Carmen Bullosa. *Journal of Latin American Cultural Studies* 4, no. 2: 145–51.

Reyes Rivas, Roxana. 1997. "Computadoras, subdesarrollo y paz." *El otro laberinto*, edited by Alvaro Zamora, 191–98. San José, Costa Rica: Editorial Tecnológica.

Robinett, Jane. 1994. *This Rough Magic: Technology in Latin American Fiction*. New York: Peter Lang.

Romero Castillo, José, Francisco Gutiérrez Carbajo, and Mario García-Page, eds. 1997. *Literatura y multimedia*. Madrid: Visor Libros.

Rose, Gillian. 1993. *Feminism and Geography: The Limits of Geographical Knowledge*. Minneapolis: University of Minnesota Press.

Sábato, Ernesto. 1968. *Uno y el universo*. Buenos Aires: Sudamericana.

Sánchez, Isidor. 1992. "Medicinas que no curan, envenenan." In *Etica, ciencia y tecnología*, edited by E. R. Ramírez and Mario Alfaro, 113–16. Cartago, Costa Rica: Editorial Tecnológica.

Sanday, Peggy Reeves. 1981. *Female Power and Male Dominance: On the Origins of Sexual Inequality.* Cambridge: Cambridge University Press.

Sarlo, Beatriz. 1994. *Escenas de la vida posmoderna: Intelectuales, arte y videocultura en la Argentina.* Buenos Aires: Ariel.

Segal, Charles. 1978. "The Menace of Dionysus: Sex Roles and Reversals in Euripides' *Bacchae.*" *Arethusa* 11: 185–202.

Shannon, Claude E., and Warren Weaver. 1964. *The Mathematical Theory of Communication.* Urbana: University of Illinois Press.

Simmons, Marlice. 1989. Concerning Rising Harm From Pesticides in the Third World. *The New York Times* 30 May: B9.

Simons, Ronald C., and Charles C. Hughes, eds. 1985. *The Culture-Bound Syndromes: Folk Illnesses of Psychiatric and Anthropological Interest.* Boston: D. Reidel.

Slater, Candace. 1994. *Dance of the Dolphin: Transformation and Disenchantment in the Amazonian Imagination.* Chicago and London: University of Chicago Press.

Sotari, Ana. 1999. "Cuento inconcluso." Online. Internet. Available http://www.chasque.apc.org/acsi/cuento.htm

Souza, Márcio. 1982. *A resistível ascenção do Boto Tucuxi.* Rio de Janeiro: Marco Zero.

Stam, Robert. 1981. *Bye Bye Brazil. Cineaste* 11, no. 1: 34–36.

Stone, Allucquére Rosanne (Sandy). 1991a. "Will the Real Body Please Stand Up?: Boundary Stories about Virtual Cultures." In *Cyberspace: First Steps*, edited by Michael Benedikt, 81–118. Cambridge, Mass.: MIT Press.

Stone, Sandy. 1991b. "The *Empire* strikes back: a Posttranssexual Manifesto." In *Body Guards: The Cultural Politics of Gender Ambiguity*, edited by Julia Epstein and Kristina Staub, 280–304. New York: Routledge.

Sutz, Judith. 1993. "The Social Implications of Information Technologies: A Latin American Perspective." In *Philosophy of Technology in Spanish Speaking Countries*, edited by Carl Mitcham, 297–308. Dordrecht, Boston, London: Kluwer.

Terceiro, José B. 1996. *Socied@d digit@l: Del homo sapiens al homo digitalis.* Madrid: Alianza.

The Dolphin [Ele o Boto]. 1987. Directed by Walter Lima Junior. Fox Lorber.

Thorndike, Lynn. 1923–77. *History of Magic and Experimental Science.* Vol. 1–8. New York: Columbia University Press.

Treichler, Paula A. 1990. "Feminism, Medicine, and the Meaning of Childbirth." In *Body/ Politics: Women and the Discourses of Science*, edited by Mary Jacobus, Evelyn Fox Keller, and Sally Shuttleworth, 113–38. New York and London: Routledge.

Trejo Delarbre, Raúl. 1996. *La nueva alfombra mágica: Usos y mitos de Internet, la red de redes.* Madrid: FUNDESCO.

Unamuno, Miguel de. 1966–71. *Obras Completas.* Madrid: Escelicer.

Vasconcelos, José. 1972. "El mestizaje." In *El ensayo en hispanoamérica*, edited by Alberto M. Vasquez, 233–48. New Orleans and Mexico: Ediciones Colibrí.

Vatá Menéndez, Juan. 1961. "La cuestión de la técnica en una doble meditación: Ortega y Heidegger." *Convivium* 9–10. 64–91. 11–12: 75–97.

Vattimo, Gianni. 1986. *El fin de la modernidad.* Translated by Alberto L. Bixio. Mexico: Gedisa.

————. 1992. *The Transparent Society.* Translated by David Webb. Baltimore: Johns Hopkins University Press.

Vernant, Jean-Pierre. 1990. *Myth and Society in Ancient Greece.* Translated by Janet Lloyd. New York: Zone Books.

Villalobos, M. L. Carlos. 1994. *Unica mirando al mar* de Fernando Contreras. *Tertulia.* 2.3 San Ramón, Costa Rica: Taller de literatura de San Ramón: 15–16.

Von Bertalanffy, Ludwig. 1987. *Teoría general de los sistemas.* Translated by Juan Almela. Mexico: Fondo de cultura económico.

Weissert, Thomas P. 1991. "Representation and Bifurcation: Borges's Garden of Chaos Dynamics." In *Chaos and Order: Complex Dynamics in Literature and Science*, ed. N. Katherine Hayles, 223–43. Chicago: University of Chicago Press.

Welch, Thomas L. and Miriam Figueras. 1982. *Travel Accounts and Descriptions of Latin America and the Caribbean, 1800–1920: A Selective Bibliography.* Washington D.C.: OAS.

Wilden, Anthony. 1987a. *Man and Women, War and Peace.* London: Routledge.

————. 1987b. *The Rules are no Game: The Strategy of Communication.* London: Routledge.

Wood, Denis. 1992. *The Power of Maps.* New York and London: Guilford Press.

Woolgar, Steve. 1988. *Science: The Very Idea.* New York and London: Routledge.

Zeitlin, Froma I. 1978. "The Dynamics of Misogyny: Myth and Mythmaking in the *Oresteia.*" *Arethusa* 2.1,2: 149–84.

Ziegfeld, Richard. 1989. "Interactive Fiction: A New Literary Genre?" *New Literary History* 20.2: 341–72.

Zimmerman, Michael E. 1990. *Heidegger's Confrontation with Modernity: Technology, Politics, Art.* Bloomington and Indianapolis: Indiana University Press.

————. 1994. *Contesting Earth's Future: Radical Ecology and Postmodernity.* Los Angeles: University of California Press.

Zum Felde, Alberto. 1954. *Indice crítico de la literatura hispanoamericana: Los ensayistas.* Mexico: Guarania.

Index